To

DO NOT REMOVE
CARDS FROM POCKET

DUNE &
OTHER WORKS

NOTES

including
- *Life of Herbert*
- *Categories of Science Fiction*
- The Book of Frank Herbert
- The Worlds of Frank Herbert
- Dune
- Dune Messiah
- *Unity & Continuity of* Dune *and* Dune Messiah
- The Godmakers
- Under Pressure
- Destination: Void
- The Eyes of Heisenberg
- The Green Brain
- The Santaroga Barrier
- Whipping Star
- Hellstrom's Hive

by
L. David Allen, M.A.
Department of English
University of Nebraska

INCORPORATED
LINCOLN, NEBRASKA 68501

Editor

Gary Carey, M.A.
University of Colorado

Consulting Editor

James L. Roberts, Ph.D.
Department of English
University of Nebraska

ISBN 0-8220-0419-4

© Copyright 1975
by
C. K. Hillegass
All Rights Reserved
Printed in U.S.A.

Cliffs Notes, Inc.   Lincoln, Nebraska

CONTENTS

LIFE AND BACKGROUND

Information, especially reliable information, about writers of science fiction is rather difficult to come by, for the great majority of them are not included in the standard sources of information about writers and other people of note. Furthermore, science-fiction novels are not always included in reference books that purport to list all books, hardback and paperback, published in the English language each year; it is also noteworthy that the card catalog in the Library of Congress does not list all of Herbert's novels. Nevertheless, some information about Herbert's life, interests, and activities is available.

Frank Herbert was born in Tacoma, Washington, in 1920. Although he had read some science fiction in scattered doses earlier in his life, Herbert did not become a serious reader of science fiction until his early twenties, some ten years before he began writing it; this, incidentally, is a contrast to the majority of science-fiction readers, many of whom report becoming avid readers by the time they were nine or ten years old. However, once he began, and especially after deciding, to try writing science fiction, he read widely and rather omnivorously, to see what had been and was being done in the field, and to get as broad a background as he could. He seems to be reluctant to name other authors from among the many whose work he has enjoyed and profited from, but H. G. Wells, Robert A. Heinlein, Jack Vance, and Poul Anderson rank very high on his list.

Herbert is a man of wide-ranging interests. For many years, his primary occupation was journalism, living in a number of places on the West Coast. In addition to journalism, however, Herbert has also worked at a variety of other professions; he has been a professional photographer, a television cameraman, a radio news commentator, a teacher of creative writing, an instructor in jungle survival, an oyster diver, and a lay analyst. He also served with the U.S. Navy during the Second World War. Of these professions, his experiences in the Navy, in jungle survival, and as a lay analyst seem to have had the greatest effect on the subject matter of his fiction. In the course of these professional experiences and in connection with his writing, Herbert has pursued a number of other interests, studying such diverse topics as undersea geology, jungle botany, navigation, anthropology, electronics, Oriental philosophy, psychology, and religion. Furthermore, he has delved deeply into ecology, lecturing on the topic and campaigning for the preservation of the world's resources; putting into practice what he preaches, Herbert has also worked with a six and one-half acre plot of land, developing it to show that a person can live a high-quality life without a huge, irreplaceable energy drain and that man can use the land in such a way that it is actually more sustaining of life when he is finished than it was before he began. As with the jobs he has held, nearly all of these other interests have found their way into his fiction; of these, however, ecology has received the greatest breadth and depth of exploration in the novels, particularly the later ones.

Herbert's many years as a journalist seem to have had a good deal of influence on the way that he works as a writer. He reports that when he is writing, he works approximately six hours each day at the typewriter— whether inspiration comes or not—and feels that there is very little difference between "worked-at writing" and "inspired writing," in the final result. In addition, his newspaper background can be detected in the fact that he keeps voluminous files on subjects of interest to him, drawing on them whenever they are appropriate to what he is writing about; sometimes the quantity of materials in his files pushes him toward writing about them, as a full file drawer of information on matters related to ecology did in the case of *Dune*.

Although Herbert began writing science fiction about twenty years ago, he had written some other fiction before that time and was interested in becoming a writer much earlier, having made the announcement that he was going to be an author the morning of his eighth birthday. What led him from this general resolve and from his attempts at "conventional fiction" cannot, he says, be precisely pinned down to any one thing, for it was a combination of many things. One of the things that he likes about science fiction is that it frees his imagination to consider many other choices and opportunities than those we seem locked into. Another is the "elbow room" it allows a writer (or reader), letting him do more interesting and divergent things with his material than he could with "mainstream" forms. Among other things, this freedom helps us to avoid either/or choices, allows us to look in relativistic directions (that is, to look at the results of any given set of conditions or premises), and makes us take a longer range view of many things, but especially of what we inflict on our world. By doing these things, science fiction can help shape our future by focusing on problems and suggesting possible results and possible alternatives in meeting them. Finally, Herbert indicates that he feels science fiction is a literary form that is rapidly gaining importance and becoming a more central element in our literary tradition.

The books discussed in these Notes are not the only ones that Herbert has produced. He has, for example, written *Threshold: The Blue Angels' Experience* (1973) about the Naval Flight team because he was fascinated by the incredible things they were doing with airplanes and by the unity of mind and body these things showed. His interest in and involvement with ecology and what we are doing to our planet led to *New World or No World* (1970), the transcripts of the *Today Show* during Earth Week 1970, which Herbert edited and provided commentary for; it provides an excellent introduction to problems which our world will encounter. *Soul Catcher*

(1972) is a sensitively written story of a young Indian who feels it necessary to sacrifice a white child, an Innocent, to join the ranks of the Innocents sacrificed by whites and thus restore the balance between the Earth and the Sky. All of these have been generally available in paperback editions. *The Heaven Makers* was reviewed, not too favorably, in the May, 1969, issue of *Venture Science Fiction;* it has not, apparently, been available since its initial publication. Finally, several of the paperback editions of his works indicate that Herbert won an International Fantasy Award for a novel published between *Under Pressure* (1956) and *Dune* (1965); this seems to be a bit of misinformation that insists on perpetuating itself, for no listing of these awards I have found contains a Herbert novel.

It is, however, his published and available science fiction, particularly *Dune,* for which Frank Herbert is noted. In addition to the discussions which follow, there are two points to be noted about this fiction. First, most of the works discussed here first saw print in various science-fiction magazines, especially *Galaxy* and *Astounding/Analog,* either as individual stories or as serials. Anyone who has access to files of such magazines might find it interesting to look at the magazine publication and compare it with the later publication in book form; several of the novels underwent rather substantial changes in this process, with *The Godmakers* being an excellent example of this change. Second, Herbert has reportedly been working on a third novel that would make *Dune* and *Dune Messiah* two-thirds of a trilogy. Although he will not talk about his work-in-progress, it seems likely that in this third novel Herbert will explore the results of the changes begun by Paul Atreides. Nevertheless, that work which he has already completed is enough to earn Herbert a permanent place in the upper echelon of science-fiction writers.

Herbert's *Dune,* on the other hand, one of the most complex yet well-integrated works of science fiction yet written, includes almost equal portions of Hard Science Fiction, Soft Science Fiction, and Science Fantasy in its make-up. The basic reference point is probably the Hard Science angle, but only because what seems to be the most satisfactory core question deals with the ecology of the planet Arrakis. Among the elements included in this aspect are the elements dealing with the planet, nearly all of which are extrapolated from current knowledge (even the sandworms are probable, based on what we know of Earth organisms of various types). The space travel, the suspensors, the weapon systems, the ornithopter, and various other gadgets also belong to the Hard Science angle, although they are speculative rather than extrapolative. Those elements which constitute the Soft Science angle include the various approaches to religion, the various approaches to physical and mental training, the Fremen way of life, the political maneuvering on the various scales, Paul's psychological development, and many other related details. Most of these things seem to be based on current knowledge, and extrapolated and re-combined. All of these elements are important in the telling of this story, and they are so well integrated that any one of them affects several others directly, and more indirectly. One example of this would be the course of Paul's development: had he not been moved to Arrakis (political), he would not have been confronted by the conditions of the planet (ecology) and thus would not have been under any pressure to develop his trained abilities nor to develop his natural powers; in the course of the novel, it is difficult to point to any event, however small, and say that only one of these things is present.

The examples are endless, and more and more science fiction is being published every day. Nevertheless, it can be safely generalized that, as the field stands now, nearly every story will be a combination of Hard Science Fiction and Soft Science Fiction, since (historically, at least) science fiction has primarily been interested in tracing the human effects of sci-entific advances and devices. Once again, it is the thinking about books and stories that is necessary to put them into such categories that is impor-tant, not the categories themselves.

CATEGORIES OF SCIENCE FICTION

Although science fiction continues to defy neat and complete defini-tion, there are a number of points which contribute toward a definition that is useful to keep in mind. These points can help suggest the general direc-tions in which science fiction seems to aim its efforts and they can also help clarify some of the things that science fiction does not aim at. Throughout the field, there seem to be two basic constants which provide guideposts, around which other points seem to cluster.

The first of these constants is that science fiction is concerned with the effects of change on human beings; this change may be brought about by the straight extrapolation of current scientific knowledge to its logical develop-ment in the near future. It may be caused by new factors that are related in some way to current science, although we cannot logically predict them at this time; we can, in other words, speculate about future developments in the sciences. Or it may be caused by simply postulating the introduction of a set of factors which are not related to current sciences at all, such as the development of psychic powers or a change in a single detail of the past. Whatever brings about the change in the conditions of life, of environment, or of mind, science fiction is primarily concerned with examining the human effects of that change.

One point related to this is that nearly any organized body of knowledge can serve for the "science" in science fiction. Although it was once popular to think of science fiction as dealing with developments in the "hard" sciences — chemistry, biology, physics, and their subdivisions, combinations, and technological applications —, more and more science fiction using such "soft" sciences as linguistics, sociology, psychology, political science, anthropology, theology, and so on, as well as that using "imaginary" sciences such as the laws of magic, time travel, and psychic powers, has been written and accepted as science fiction. One thing that all of these have in common is the fact that they are all *organized* ways of knowing something.

Another point related to this first constant is that science fiction is a literary sub-genre of prose fiction in which some kind of science happens to be an important part. An important fact to remember is that when some aspect of science and some aspect of literature, such as telling the story, characterization, or theme, come in conflict, it is the science that will be modified most. Of course, most writers of science fiction try to be as accurate as possible about their science, but sometimes it must be de-emphasized or hedged a bit if the novel or story as a whole is to work. One instance of this point is *Dune*. The over-all plan, or the steps needed, for changing the planet might be fascinating, but for Herbert to have gone into detail about this would have gotten in the way of telling the story and of other elements in the novel.

The second constant, which is basic to both science and science fiction, is the assumption that we live in an orderly universe; this is important, because it means that the causes of changed conditions can be discovered and explained and that the results will be regular and, within limits, predictable. For example, in *Whipping Star*, McKie and the Caleban cannot communicate in any meaningful way at the beginning of the novel; however, McKie continues to attempt to communicate because he knows that languages have underlying conceptual systems that have form and pattern, and he believes that if he and the Caleban talk long enough, one or the other of them may gather sufficient data to grasp that system, with a resulting increase in communication.

Even with these constants and related points, science fiction is a broad field covering many possible materials, many possible approaches to those materials, and many possible ways of handling them. For this reason, many people find it sometimes helpful to have some kind of categories and sub-categories to help them sort things out. However, it is important to remember that any label chooses some aspect of a work to emphasize and plays down all the rest of the work; consequently, if such labels and the process of sticking them on becomes an end in itself, rather than a momentary convenience, the richness and worth of the literary work is virtually destroyed. Furthermore, any set of labels can never be final and any application of any set will depend in part on a personal point of view. With these cautions in mind, the following set of categories for science fiction are suggested.

The first category, then, might be called Hard Science Fiction. This would be science fiction in which the major impetus for the exploration which takes place is one of the so-called Hard, or Physical, Sciences, including chemistry, physics, biology, astronomy, geology, and possibly mathematics, as well as the technology associated with, or growing out of, one of those sciences. Such sciences, and consequently any science fiction based on them, assume the existence of an orderly universe whose laws are regular and discoverable.

A second general category can be labeled Soft Science Fiction. This encompasses science fiction in which the major impetus for the exploration is one of the so-called Soft Sciences—that is, sciences focusing on human activities, most of which have not been fully accepted as being as rigorous or as capable of prediction as the physical sciences. Soft Science Fiction would include any stories based on such organized approaches to knowledge as sociology, psychology, anthropology, political science, historiography, theology, linguistics, and some approaches to myth. Stories about any technology related to these would also come under this heading. In this category, as well, the assumption of an orderly universe with regular, discoverable laws is a basic criterion for inclusion.

A third category that seems required is Science Fantasy. Under this heading would go those stories which, assuming an orderly universe with regular and discoverable natural laws, propose that the natural laws are different from those we derive from our current sciences. What is sometimes called paraphysics, but especially those branches dealing with telepathy and the laws of magic, most often provides these alternative laws. To qualify as Science Fantasy, it is necessary that these alternate laws receive at least a minimum of direct exploration. There are, however, some complications to this, which will be discussed when these categories are broken into sub-categories.

The final category, Fantasy, is somewhat controversial, for its connection with any of the sciences, as such, is minimal. Nevertheless, it borders on science fiction and helps round out this system of categories. As it is used here, Fantasy has this much in common with the other categories: it, too, assumes a universe which has order and a set of discoverable natural laws, even though they are different from our own. Unlike Science Fantasy, where these laws are treated explicitly, in Fantasy these laws are merely implicit—that is, if the reader is sufficiently interested, he can formulate the laws governing this fantasy world, but the author gives him little or no assistance in doing so in any direct way.

One should note, here, that among Herbert's works, which are largely

Soft Science Fiction, *Under Pressure* provides an example of both Hard Science Fiction and Soft Science Fiction. The general setting is a world that has been at war for some time (which, when it was published, was a projection of the "Cold War") and which is desperately in need of oil, which is fast running out (an ecological and geological projection—hard science—which is rapidly being substantiated). The government has moved toward repression and total control; this kind of "soft science" projection can be seen in embryo during most wars. The submarines are somewhat advanced beyond those we had in 1956, but not a great deal; to bring this technological—hard science—extrapolation into being, only a few steps beyond current knowledge and technology is needed. Finally, the psychology (soft science) applied in the book is more or less current, but projected into a somewhat different context; in addition, there is an extrapolation of both a growing importance for psychology and psychologists in government agencies and an increasing use of technological gadgets in psychological diagnosis and treatment, both of which seem reasonable projections, given current trends. Thus, *Under Pressure* would lie between the poles of Hard Science Fiction and Soft Science Fiction, leaning toward the "soft" end of the spectrum because the central exploration of the novel deals with the psychology of the men in the submarine.

THE BOOK OF FRANK HERBERT
(DAW Books, Inc., 1973)

THE WORLDS OF FRANK HERBERT
(Ace Books, 1971)

These two collections of Herbert's shorter fiction, reprints of stories that had appeared earlier in various science-fiction magazines, share both the virtues and the weaknesses of all such anthologies. The major weakness, of course, is the fact that the stories are not of equal quality, ranging from the very lightweight and simple to the relatively complex, from adequate presentation and characterization to very good. However, the virtues outweigh the weaknesses by a considerable margin. Perhaps the most important virtue is that these nineteen stories, which would otherwise be virtually inaccessible to most readers, but especially to those who have recently taken to reading science fiction or who do not live near a library which collects the magazines in which these stories appeared, have been brought together in two volumes; for anyone who has found Herbert's other works interesting and worth reading, this is a worthwhile service. Another point of interest, one that will be most important in discussing these stories, is the way in which they interact with one another and with the novels, dealing with themes and ideas, and even characters, that appear elsewhere. Thus these stories provide a basis from which to view some of the themes and ideas to which Herbert consistently returns in his writings and from which to look at the variations and permutations in them as they appear in different contexts.

"Seed Stock," the first story in *The Book of Frank Herbert* (these stories will be discussed in the order in which they are found in the books, beginning, first, with *The Book of Frank Herbert* and, later, with *The Worlds of Frank Herbert*), is certainly one of the best and most significant stories in these two volumes. Its subject is the mutual adaptation of humans to a new planet and of the planet to humans. The most obvious conflict in this story is between mankind and the planet which he is attempting to settle and colonize; equally important, however, is the conflict between the scientists and the laborers, with the technicians caught in the middle and carrying the balance of power. Both conflicts involve the *way* in which the adaptations will take place; this is the thematic focus for the story, which is really a character study of Kroudar (a laborer) and his wife Honida (a technician) that emphasizes their relationship to the land. The scientists insist that the planet should adapt to humans, that the plants and animals brought from Earth should be able to thrive here; yet the scientists are also portrayed as being somewhat mentally stagnant; they are unable to explain why the new conditions of this planet produce the effects they do, and they are unable to wrench themselves free of old patterns of thought in a new situation to find new answers. Kroudar, the embodiment of the slow-witted, physically able worker, represents the antithesis of the scientists' approach toward this new planet. He has begun to "feel" with this new world; he has sensed the particular "rhythms" of the land and the sea, but he can barely communicate what he feels—except by action. Honida is a technician, the bridge between the two groups; she is able to understand both the scientists and Kroudar, to draw knowledge from them, and to put it to work—that is, in her genetic research (the method she uses) the theoretical techniques which she uses are those of the scientists. But she is more curious than the scientists and thus she produces a new variety of corn because of her "feeling" for the new land. This facet of her character, we realize, was the basis for her choosing Kroudar as her mate, made against the wishes of the scientists; the reader is left quite certain that their children, their line, will have the best chances of surviving and flourishing. Thus, although it is suggested that the intuition has a better chance for survival than pure intellect, survival is better enhanced by the two forces in human life working in concert. The same is true of the conflict between adapting oneself to the planet and adapting the planet to oneself: a combination of these, a compromise, is the most likely to be successful.

"The Nothing" is perhaps not quite as complex or as significant as

"Seed Stock," but it is an interesting and compact story which raises some of the issues which are explored in more detail in several of the novels. Strangely enough, the basic pattern is the girl-meets-boy story that we have read for years. Jean Carlysle, because of an argument with her father, goes down to the tavern for a drink and to talk about jobs; a good-looking young man (Claude Williams) comes in and sits down beside her; she tries to strike up a conversation; the police enter and take her and Claude to his father, a VIP; he approves of her; they get married; she goes home to get her things; when she returns, she reaffirms her decision to be married.

In one sense, this plot is similar to those stories in the *Saturday Evening Post* in the 1940s. However, the society in which this story takes place and the problem to be solved overshadow this simple story line. The story itself takes place sometime in the future, several generations after an atomic war, the radiation from which has produced a number of mutations. All these mutations, at least those mentioned in the story, are mental, involving the development of such psi-powers as telepathy, teleportation, prescience, and the ability to set fires with a glance. On the other hand, there are the Nothings, those who have none of these psi-powers; there are a number of preserves, apparently for the protection of the Nothings, but also (rather secretly) a place to preserve and develop the pre-Talent era means of doing things. Jean is a "pyro," with flashes of telepathy; Mensor Williams is one of only nine people who have all the Talents to a very high degree of proficiency, but his son Claude is a Nothing. The postulated problem, which brings Claude and Jean into marriage, is that the Talents are becoming dulled with each generation and that more and more children are being born without Talents. The biological basis for this is the fact that extremes from the norm tend to produce toward the average — that is, those who are geniuses *tend* to have children who are less intelligent or less talented than their parents. What this means is that, although the Talents will probably never die out, a rather drastic change must soon take place in society. The preserves are doing two things: re-establishing the pre-Talent ways of doing things and matching gene charts to find those with the greatest chances of producing Talented children; this latter purpose is a primary reason for Mensor Williams's urging the marriage between Claude and Jean, for there is a seventy percent chance that their children will be telepathic, prescient, or both. There is also the added twist that beyond a certain point, rapidly approaching, the prescients cannot see; nearly everything about Claude and Jean, for example, is a "blank" to Mensor Williams, which is rather unusual but a relief to Jean, especially because of her wedding night. Behind all of this, presented indirectly and by means of suggestions rather than in detail, is the society, which is clear and fascinating in its own right; to give only one example, one simply asks if someone is a teleporter and visualizes the destination when one wants to go somewhere.

Herbert's "Rat Race" is based on that hoary and overworked science-fiction premise of aliens being secretly among us, but he has managed an interesting treatment of the idea, primarily by turning it into a detective story. Welby Lewis, chief of criminal investigation under Sheriff John Czernak in a fairly large town, goes to a mortuary to deliver a bottle of stomach washings to the county hospital. When he gets there, a number of things puzzle him, which leads him to try and collect some solid facts to confirm his suspicions. He and a deputy observe the place, and Welby decides to question a Mr. Johnson, one of the owners of the mortuary. Johnson panics, decides that he must do something to prevent Welby's discovery, and shoots him; only the fact that Welby's heart is on the wrong side saves him (this freakish placement was carefully established early in the story). Johnson then commits suicide. With Welby in the hospital, other people keep bringing in information, pieces in the puzzle. The end result is that they discover that aliens have been using human beings as test animals in a variety of ways. But whereas many stories stop at this point, Herbert continues with his central question: what does one do with test animals when he discovers that they are intelligent and have discovered what one is doing — and what will aliens do with us, now that we have discovered their operations? Dr. Bellarmine decides that he will be the volunteer to try and contact the aliens and be the first volunteer for their psychological testing. A symbolic communication is sent back from the aliens that shows their awareness of our awareness and an apparent willingness to discontinue this stage of their experimentation. The process of suspicion, investigation, hypothesis, and tentative verification is the main interest in "Rat Race," as it is in most detective stories or in any problem-solving story. The conclusions arrived at, and the bases for them, are what distinguish this story from mere science fiction. Whereas in the first two stories the setting was used to mark the differences from life on Earth as we know it now, Herbert has tried in this story to make the setting real and ordinary to both counter-act and accentuate the conclusions of the characters. The technique for presenting this background is, however, the same as in most of these stories: key details and suggestions are suggested rather than detailed. For example, many people have seen offices in older court houses, and the details which are provided for Sheriff Czernak's office — a radiator, a pinup calendar, stained and flaking plaster walls, beat-up desks, etc. — are designed to remind readers and let them fill in the rest of the details. Finally, there is one thematic item which is brought out near the end of the story that should be noted. This is the idea that pure scientists of any race would follow the human pattern and would be able to control themselves, which the characters take to mean that they would be able to understand the problems of other beings. Johnson, the alien who panicked, is probably a lab man or a field technician and, thus, is not as highly trained or as disinterested as a pure scientist might be; the characters also suggest that he is not even a good technician, for he has made too many mistakes.

"Gambling Device" is a gimmick story, interesting but rather light-weight. Because they missed a turn, a newly-wed couple arrives at the Desert Rest Hotel, where no gambling is allowed; once they are in their room, a voice explains that here nothing is left to chance; that they have the security of pre-determination, and that free choice has been eliminated—totally. This means, among other things, that no one can talk unless they have made, in advance, a conscious decision to do so. The couple wishes to leave, so the husband creates a gamble that will necessarily make the hotel a part of it; the hotel, only a machine and not programmed for such things, has to remove itself, leaving them outside and free to go on their way.

"Looking for Something?" is similar to "Rat Race" in that it deals with aliens using us in much the same way that we use animals; here, however, little has been done to refresh an old idea, although the story is not badly written. The idea is that aliens are controlling human perception of reality so that they can obtain a fluid they call "korad," which confers immortality on them—and would for us—if we could keep it. The story is told from the point of view of a Denebian administrator making a report about an error, in which a hypnotist glimpsed the true reality, what is happening and how it came about.

"The Gone Dogs" is one of the three best stories in *The Book of Frank Herbert*. The story, and the chain-reaction that follows, begins when a rancher-veterinarian, planning to wipe out his coyote problem, releases a female coyote infected with a mutated hog cholera virus. Unfortunately, while it is effective for the coyotes, the disease spreads to other canines and becomes anerobic, as well as being carried by humans, who release the virus through their sweat glands. With the removal of coyotes and dogs, other predators (wolves and foxes) that had been kept in check by the canines begin to be a problem. In addition, as dogs become more scarce, people begin to do strange things in order to save the dogs they have or to get a dog to replace one which died; many dogs are put on spaceships to be taken to other planets to keep them safe, only to be dumped by the crews—after they have taken the money.

Tragically, the last dogs on Earth are killed by a woman who decides that she *must* have a dog and, consequently, defies nearly impassable territory and evades robot guards to get to a dog preserve. Not only does this situation have ecological and human effects but also political and even interplanetary effects.

The Vegans, with whom Earth has been on friendly terms for some time and who are far ahead of Earth's scientists in bio-physics, are extremely proud of their *mikeses* generator, which allows cross-breeding between different species. Earth, however, refuses to allow the Vegans to have dogs because of their experiments on the animals; by implication, this attitude is representative of many other elements in the relationships between the two races. Finally, the Vegans withdraw from all contact with Earth when the dogs are smuggled to them by Dr. Varley Trent. The dogs, however, are "special" dogs: they have the familiar beagle head and brown and white fur—but all have six legs. Thus the story is a step-by-step look at the consequences of a single act, at the discoveries that are made in the process of analyzing what has happened, and at the attempts to do something about the situation, both legal and non-legal. The quality of the story is due to the interest of the problem postulated, the number of facets of the problem which are explored, and the unity of the whole.

"Passage for Piano" focuses on the human aspects of preparing for colonizing a new planet by examining the problems of one family as they choose what they will take. The Hatchell family seems to be an excellent choice for both the purposes of the story and the purposes of colonization: Walter Hatchell is the chief ecologist of the expedition, an expert in setting up the delicate balance of growing things to support human life on an alien world; his wife is a nurse-dietician; their two children are precocious and very talented. The problem of the story develops from the fact that each adult can take only seventy-five pounds of luggage and each child under fourteen can take only forty pounds. With Walter and with Rita, the daughter, there seems to be very little problem, for they are not particularly attached to things or items. Mrs. Hatchell, on the other hand, is quite attached to things and has been having some difficulty in choosing what to take, and she is gradually beginning to panic. The real difficulty is with their son, David, who is a blind piano prodigy who has full concert stature at the age of twelve. (One of the interesting clusters of details indicates that his blindness is the result of a rare illness brought back by an exploratory expedition; it has also apparently left his emotional balance somewhat off-center.) He is upset because he cannot take his piano with him (it weighs fourteen hundred and eight pounds); the psychiatrist believes that David could die without it, and that the very least that might happen is the destruction of his talent, for he *feels* a connection between the piano and his talent as legacies of his grandfather. Walter's position makes it virtually impossible, particularly at the point that has been reached in preparing, for them to consider staying behind. Mrs. Hatchell figures that if each of the three hundred and eight colonists contributes just four pounds and twelve ounces, they can take the piano; before Charlesworthy, the leader of the expedition, learns of this unauthorized plan, she has collected five hundred and fifty-four pounds and eight ounces. When Charlesworthy finally telephones Margaret to confirm the matter, David proposes the workable compromise, taking only the keyboard & the strings, with the rest to be made on the new planet; as he says, it will then be part of both worlds. The leader commits himself and his wife to contributing eight and one-half pounds allowance needed to take the "piano." This is a rather quiet story, but it seems very real and has a solid impact. One important factor in producing both this sense of reality and its impact is the fact that Herbert takes some time to show that David is *not* simply throwing a temper tantrum about the piano; the roots of his problem are much deeper, most of them unconscious. For example, when his mother decides to find a way to take the piano, he is unhappy about leaving the piano behind but he is also unhappy about asking people to give up some of their precious belongings so that he can take it; furthermore, he is the one who suggests, without prompting from any source, the compromise that saves both him and enriches the colony. Finally, although the situation is not as severe when the Atreides family must move from Caladan to Arrakis, this story has a great deal in common with the first part of *Dune* and can help us understand the feelings of all those who have been uprooted, but especially those of Jessica; the importance of psychological roots is also seen in the last part of *The Godmakers*.

One of the ideas that recurs frequently in Herbert's short stories is the emphasis on the *human* effects of, or on *human* reactions to, the various kinds of changes in the situation that he explores. This, in spite of some awkwardness in the handling and presentation, is the virtue of such a story as "Encounter in a Lonely Place." In the story, an older man who has held himself apart from the life of the village in which his family has lived for several generations tells a younger man, a writer wounded in the war, who has come back to the town where his grandparents had lived to recuperate, about his ability to read *a* mind. At the age of seventeen, he fell in love with a servant girl who worked for his sister. One night they were playing a card game, and he named every card that she turned up without looking at them; ever since, he has seen things through "her eyes." Unfortunately, this woman, the only woman he ever loved, thinks that he is some kind of demon and will not marry him. Although, in summary, this idea may seem contrived, Herbert's dramatization makes it seem real and effective. The man also reveals much the same kind of loneliness and struggle in coping with his gift/curse as Paul Atreides experienced in *Dune* and, to a lesser extent, Lewis Orne in *The Godmakers*.

"Operation Syndrome" is probably the best story in this collection; it is also one of the most fully balanced science-fiction stories, along with "Seed Stock" and "The Gone Dogs," bringing together psychological exploration, discovery of a new device, the process of problem solving in both these areas, and the human effects of both. The first paragraph, plus two one-line paragraphs, sets the problem in general terms, focusing briefly on Honolulu, the first of nine cities hit by the Scramble Syndrome. For years, they have been peaceful and normal; suddenly, the entire city is insane, almost totally. Other such brief views, each of a different city, are scattered throughout the story. The scene then shifts to Seattle, focusing on Dr. Eric Ladde, a psychiatrist who is having a dream. It later becomes clear that his dream is of Colleen Lanai and the musikron. The project on which he is working, and has been working on unsuccessfully for some time, is the construction of a teleprobe, a machine to interpret encephalographic waves to communicate with the unconscious mind.

The next morning, he meets Colleen Lanai and recognizes her from his dream. He strikes up a conversation with her, and two processes are set in motion: they gradually fall in love, and, more important, the cause and nature of the Scramble Syndrome is discovered. Finally, the knowledge that the Scramble Syndrome is tied to the musikron and sets in twenty-eight hours after it leaves a city is established. Furthermore, Pete Serantis developed the machine while working with Dr. Carlos Amanti, who is in an insane asylum and who was Dr. Ladde's teacher and originator of the idea of a teleprobe. Ladde's theory is that the musikron funnels disturbing impulses directly into the unconscious; after a time, the mind cannot handle the resonances, and insanity results. Because these impulses reach everyone, except a very few who are immune or prepared, within a certain radius, the results are disastrous. The love story is complicated by the presence of Pete Serantis, a man twisted physically and mentally, who is insanely jealous of Colleen Lanai. When Colleen first attempts to give Eric the plans to the musikron so he can compare them with his teleprobe and perhaps find out what is hindering its development, Pete deliberately substitutes plans that would destroy anyone who would apply them as found. Later, even though she feels guilty about betraying Pete and will not believe that he had anything to do with whatever is causing the Scramble Syndrome, she does leave the real plans behind when they leave for London. From them, Eric and an assistant recruited at the last moment, build a functional teleprobe, although it is finally finished four hours after the Syndrome has hit; he has sent his assistant away before the Syndrome occurs, and he himself is only lightly affected because of his training, his work with the teleprobe, and his expectation that it would occur. When he finishes the teleprobe, he uses it to probe for the minds of others trained in psychology, gradually building up a network that can then move outward to calm the minds of the general population. At the end of the story, Colleen returns to him.

Many of the things that make this a fine and interesting story, of course, are not dwelt on in this appraisal. One of these is the construction of the teleprobe; we are given a sense that it would be possible to build one by the quotations from books by Amanti, by the discussions of circuit diagrams and the parts needed, and the descriptions of putting the instrument together (which also provides a sense of the time and urgency involved).

Another, perhaps the most interesting aspect of the story, is the exploration of the mind working when Dr. Ladde first puts on the teleprobe and moves, first, into some of the hidden areas of his own mind and then into the minds of others. Finally, there are such touches as the almost casual mention of things that would be taken for granted in a future society and the interactions of the characters. All of these combine to make a rich, complex, and interesting story.

The device of using an unexpected twist for an ending and the element of satire on our readiness to find a military solution for problems provide the interest in the last story in this collection, "Occupation Force." A huge alien spaceship is sighted over the United States. A high-level conference is called to decide what to do about it, with many of those present believing it to be a mission of conquest and ready to use the "Bomb," especially after it is reported that an Earthman has been taken aboard. However, it is decided that a peaceful means will be tried first, though military precautions will be held in immediate readiness. The general who is appointed to greet the aliens has his suspicions aroused by various references to a colonial program by the alien's ambassador. He refers, of course, to their colonization of Earth — seven thousand years ago.

The first story in *The Worlds of Frank Herbert*, "The Tactful Saboteur," is a fun story with several serious underlying themes. Much of the fun is due to the antics of Jorj X. McKie in his capacity of Saboteur Extraordinary; anyone and anything, with only a few limitations, are fair game. On a more serious level, there is a need for a government to be slow working in order to protect the rights of private citizens; it is for the purpose of slowing things down that the Bureau of Sabotage was formed in the first place. According to McKie, once in the past, red tape was eliminated from the workings of government; it then slipped into high gear and began moving even faster, with laws passed within an hour of conception, appropriations coming and going in a fortnight, new bureaus coming into being almost on whim, and so on. Thus the bureau functions to slow things down, to incite disputes and battles between agencies to expose the temperamental types who can't control themselves and think on their feet, to keep the public entertained and fascinated by their flamboyant obstructionism, to stir up opposition between political parties on the theory that it tends to expose reality, and to provide an outlet for society's troublemakers. However, it is also made clear that indiscriminate obstruction is not desirable. Some government agencies are apparently immune from sabotage all the time, and others some of the time under specified conditions; only the Bureau of Sabotage is *never* immune. In fact, the way to advance in the Bureau is through successful sabotage against one's superiors. In addition, one of their axioms is that the bigger a project is, the more attention it should get from the Bureau.

Another of these more serious themes is the inter-relationships between various sentient beings. Although several others are mentioned, the two main types focused on are humans and the Pan-Spechi. In the course of an investigation for the Bureau, it becomes necessary for Jorj X. McKie to probe beneath the commonly known facts that the Pan-Spechi are a five-gendered race in which ego-dominance passes periodically from one to another member of a creche (their basic five member unit) to find out as much as possible about their creche life and ego-transfer. This is complicated by the fact that these are among the most private elements of Pan-Spechi life, and that the Pan-Spechi have rather rigorous requirements about the propriety of conversations about them; talking about the creche could easily lead to immediate death. It is a tribute to McKie's courage, sensitivity, knowledge, and tact that he manages to reveal these things without getting killed. As he points out near the end of the story, these two races and cultures have lived together in *apparent* understanding for centuries; only *now* are they really attempting to understand each other, to find out the values and systems of meaning that are most basic to each culture, without which mutual understanding and respect are virtually impossible.

In both "The Tactful Saboteur" and the story which follows it, "By the Book," a problem is postulated, data is gathered, and a solution is arrived at; nevertheless, they are quite different stories, for while the problem and the exploration in "The Tactful Saboteur" deals with cultural and semantic materials, "By the Book" deals with technological materials. "By the Book" postulates that an angle-space transmission beam has been developed. Through angle-space, the theory goes, every place in the universe is just around the corner from every other place. Although scientists have developed a beam that sends things through angle-space when conditions are right, they are not sure just how it works or exactly what happens at the other end, and they are just now developing the mathematics to explain the phenomena involved; this, of course, is often the way that scientific discovery proceeds. Using the angle-space transmissions, humans have sent out containers with human and animal embryos toward new, inhabitable worlds. These containers have everything necessary to care for the embryos once they land, with gestation vats, mechanical "nursemaids" and educational systems, materials for development, and so on. However, the farther away the containers, the muddier the contact with them, and the more uncertain their fate becomes. Thus, the Haigh Company, and its best troubleshooter, Ivar Norris Gump, must find out what is clouding contact and how to insure the safe arrival of the containers; before the story begins, six other troubleshooters have died trying to solve these problems. Much of the story, then, is a description of the beam tube hollowed out of rock on the moon and of the process of examining the situation and gathering data that Gump goes through. Finally, he develops a hypothesis and convinces the company to build him a container that will allow him to test this hypothesis and to be sent out along the beam. His theory is borne out, and he provides data that will change the mathematics and the theories being developed to explain the beam and its actions toward greater accuracy; in addition, he is in a position to help guide the containers down, and he has suggested the means to have others come through to help *and* return to Earth. Gump, however, has decided that he would like to stay. Thus, the process of the scientific method provides the major interest of the story, but it does not lack the human element. One of the nicer touches, in fact, is the way that Gump uses the rule books; he has one of the finest collections of them, including some very old ones. He often quotes from them, but many times he refers also to the fact that they were written by people far from the situation they are supposed to be applied in. He uses these choice quotations for many purposes: to amuse himself, to get things done by quoting their own words back to the company's board, to help himself sort out his thinking, and to determine a point from which to approach a problem; finally, he senses that the value of handbooks is to provide a sense of order and system, and to protect man against chaos.

"Committee of the Whole" could take place at just about anytime, for the change that the story postulates is very slight, and very little (if any) new knowledge or technology would be needed to bring it about. The main focus of the story is the revolutionary impact that a single, rather simple, device could have on our society. Part of the interest of this story is the satiric portrait of a Senate Committee in action, with a particular focus on the chairman, who is attempting to twist matters to his advantage and who will throw his weight around if necessary to do so; this Senate hearing provides the frame of the story, the situation in which the device is introduced. Another part of the interest is the fact that William R. Custer, the prime witness before the Committee, can out-think the Senator and refuses to let things be twisted; in addition, he knows he has something which can put a stop to the kind of power games which the Senator is trying to play.

The third point of interest in this story is the technological gadget that Custer introduces before the Committee — and to the world, through the television coverage of the hearing. This device is a homemade laser, which Custer explains very fully, including the materials and the process involved in making one; the materials are easily found, with many substitutions possible, and nearly anyone who is interested could make one. Custer has used this opportunity to broadcast the details of this device because he feels that the power over people's actions is becoming far too concentrated in too few people, whose interest is in preserving that power and in playing power games; the Committee chairman illustrates the point very well.

Ultimately, then, Custer's concern is for the dignity of individual human beings; he feels that his device will introduce an element which will force every human to consider the dignity of every other human. However, he is not purely an idealist, for he recognizes that there will be no period of violence as the change in behavior is made, but he is sufficiently an idealist to believe that mankind will survive and emerge strengthened and moving in a more positive direction. It is interesting to note that *all* of Herbert's novels are concerned in some way with the question of the ways in which governments use their power; most of the novels postulate either some way to subvert that power or some means of limiting its effects.

The central target of "Mating Call" is human ignorance, our feeling that we must uplift the ignorant and backward beings in our world (our universe), our self-centered definitions of ignorance and backwardness, and our tendency to act before we know all the facts. The problem to be solved, which forms the framework of the story, is that the birthrate on Rukuchp has been reduced since the introduction of foreign music to that planet. Marie Medill, a young woman with a doctorate in music, and Laoconia Wilkinson, a senior field agent of the Social Anthropological Service who is tone deaf, are sent to the planet to implement Marie's plan to teach the natives more about our musical forms; they are escorted by a full crew in space.

This plan has been accepted because music seems to have something to do with the process of conception and birth on Rukuchp, although the humans have never found out exactly what the relationship is or how the natives reproduce. The contrast between these two agents provides most of the thematic thrust of the story, for Marie Medill has a great deal of sympathy for these natives and has taken the trouble to begin to recognize them as individuals, while Laoconia, the professional, views them simply as specimens to be put through a battery of tests without regard to individuality or dignity—mere creatures to have her opinions and beliefs imposed on. In addition, Marie doubts the wisdom of what they are about to do and wishes to refrain until they have more complete information; Laoconia, on the other hand, insists on going ahead once she has made up her mind. Because Laoconia is the professional and the senior member of the group, her decision is final; as a result, all the women who hear the natives' Big Sing reproduce parthenogenically, as in cell division. Because this event is transmitted back to the ship, this includes all the women in the crew; because the concert was pirated and rebroadcast, it includes nearly all women who are capable of conceiving. Thus are the tables turned on the originators of a hasty and potentially disastrous action, rather than wiping out the recipients, as the story indicates happened to one race just before this story opens.

"Escape Felicity" concerns Roger Deirut, a D-ship man exploring the universe of places habitable by man. The first part of the story focuses on Deirut's struggle to overcome the "Push," a compulsion to turn around and go home, which grows stronger as the D-ship pilots get farther from Earth. He believes (wrongly) that the Bu-psych operators are responsible for this, to make sure the pilots return to let them know about any finds or information. This belief is one of the devices that he uses to keep himself going, to keep from turning back; this part of the story records the basics of the methods he uses to stay out ninety-four days, breaking Bingaling's record of eighty-one days. On the ninety-fourth day, he emerges from the hydrogen cloud that has defeated other pilots and he finds a planet .998 of Earth norm. Particularly in view of the end of the story, this constitutes a brief study of man's ability to rationalize his discoveries. The largest part of the story deals with his contact with the aliens inhabiting this planet. To a major degree, this contact is a mutual exploration of each other's language. Deirut uses the ship's computer; the aliens translate mentally. Although the world and the aliens with whom he comes in contact seem very primitive and pastoral to Deirut, their civilization is twenty-five million years old and even these simple shepherds have abilities far beyond Deirut's understanding.

Finally the aliens sit around, mentally altering Deirut's memory and that of the ship and intensifying the "Push." He is then sent on his way home, dreaming of, someday, finding a planet like the one he has just left, proud of his ninety-four days out, and wondering why the force he feels is called the "Push" instead of the "Pull." The story makes it clear that this has happened many times in the past and suggests that, contrary to our expectations, we really have very little to offer other intelligent beings. This is a fine reversal of a great many alien contact stories and makes an interesting complement to "Mating Call."

"The GM Effect" might be the other side of "Committee of the Whole," a view of what might have happened if Custer had *not* made sure that his invention received wide publicity. First, two of the developers of the GM effect gather together everyone who has had anything to do with developing or experimenting with it—or who knows anything at all about it. They then find a convenient excuse to leave, for the others are to be destroyed by soldiers. They obviously feel that they are safe from any action against them, though one felt the possibility of some kind of action and tried to get out some copies of the formula and to hide others. However, the Brigadier General in charge of the operation anticipated him and intercepted or found all these copies. The two conspirators are shot, and the General implies that all the soldiers involved in this operation will be effectively silenced. He retains the only copy of the formula, as well as some of the information gained from the experiments, both of which he intends to use in further power games. The "hows" of the effect are never explained. Working from the Jungian concept of racial memory, Herbert postulates that this liquid (even this is not clearly the case) unlocks in an individual the memories of his ancestors in the direct line: Father A, Mother B, Grandfathers and Grandmothers A and B, and so on. In addition, he suggests that, at least for a time, there is a dual awareness of oneself in the present and the past of one's ancestors. The first thing that occurs to the scholars who developed the GM effect is that it will change history as a written record, for they discover ancestors who were involved in important events. In addition, they can find out the backgrounds of people, the hiding places of secret records, and so on, because of the over-lap between people with the same ancestors. Whereas the academics see this information as changing history, the General sees it as a lever that can be used to increase his power. This seems to be exactly what would have happened with Custer's laser tool/weapon had he not broadcast instructions about it to the world before those in power could stop him.

"The Featherbedders" is rather nicely summed up by the quote from Swift that ends the story: "A flea hath smaller fleas that on him prey; and these have smaller still to bite 'em; and so proceed *ad infinitum.*" The story is about two Slorin, both of whom have effectively blended into Earth society and have found their niche. They are on a mission to find out about a set of events and mental disturbances which suggest something very much like a Slorin gone wild and revealing himself. They find him, one who was injured in the forced landing of their ship on Earth, and who has only a partial memory of who he is, what he is, and how he should be behaving. Although it isn't revealed until the end, the village on which the damaged Slorin has been imposing law and order is completely composed of other beings who prey on the Slorin; they forced the landing of the Slorin ship so they could use it, and they usually wait until the Slorin have moved in before they move in themselves. The story is filled with aphorisms, etc., about how to be an effective parasite. The Slorin can take, for example, any form to at least seventy-five percent accuracy. But whereas the Slorin tend toward bureaucratic roles, the other race works further down the economic ladder, as peasants, common people, and so on. The Slorin also believe it to be imperative to avoid nudging humans to an awareness of their existence and the development of undeveloped powers, and the other race feels exactly the same about the Slorin. Furthermore, actually filling the niche they have selected, rather than just "acting" at it is a prime directive of the Slorin, as is moderation in all things. Because these two directives are not going hand-in-hand at the village is the reason for Slorin concern and investigation. In a way, then, this story is a handbook for fitting oneself into a system, of adapting oneself to the system and slowly changing it; with very little difficulty, it can be applied to humans and their relationship with Earth's ecosystem, showing the errors of the incomplete and undisciplined approach and the possibilities of a better approach.

"Old Rambling House" is another story in which hasty action based on an incomplete view of the consequences leads to an undesirable conclusion. On the surface, it is a story about swapping an old rambling house for a trailer house. The couple with the trailer is very anxious to have the house, but they are a little suspicious about getting something for next to nothing; in the end, their greed convinces them to ignore their suspicions, just as the couple with the house planned. The couple with the house seems only interested in getting rid of the house. After the Grahams decide to take the house, something strange happens and the "stinger" in the deal is explained. The Rushes, the former inhabitants of the house, were subjects of the Rojac, tax collectors conditioned so they could not leave the job, but clever enough to find assenting substitutes. The house is a kind of space conveyance travelling along the collection route; the irony is that travel and rootlessness is precisely what the Grahams were trying to escape. The Rojac, from the little information given in the story, are strong believers in the Puritan ethic; they are severe, hard-working, against such frivolity as poetry, and so on. Furthermore, they are always looking for new inhabitable places. The final shock is that the Rushes discover that because Mrs. Graham is pregnant, and because the unborn child did not participate in the decision, Mr. Rush will feel compelled to call the Rojac at the time of decision, confess—and thus give them another planet to take over. Because two couples acted hastily, Earth has eighteen years before take-over.

"A-W-F Unlimited," the final story in *The Worlds of Frank Herbert*, is a love story, a problem-solving story, and a story of a confrontation with people playing power games, all neatly tied together with a background that satirizes advertising and the world it is strangling. The problem to be solved, around which all the rest revolves, is that the enlistments in WOMS (Women of Space) have fallen to nearly zero. The advertising firm of Singlemaster, Hucksting and Battlemont has been chosen by the military to find out why this has happened and, as a result, to create a way to reverse this trend; as an incentive, suggested by Psych Branch, the entire male membership of the company will be drafted if a solution is not found. One complication is the fact that Gwen Everest (note the name), who has been the problem-solving genius of the firm for twenty-two years, is beginning to detest the world which she has helped create and she is beginning to lose control of herself; for example, as she comes to work one morning, amidst the ever-present advertising that she has created, instead of tuning it out, she uses a code word which sends an advertising robot out of control and it destroys itself. A second complication is Brigadier General Sonnet Finnister of WOMS, an unattractive woman who has designed the uniform of WOMS to mask her own physical deficiencies, even though it looks hideous on every other member of the service. This uniform and the space armor, the military has discovered, seem to be the cause of the dropping enlistments. The story makes it quite obvious that Gwen would normally react to people like Generals Finnister and Owling in much the same way as she does under any circumstances, but it also makes it clear that this time she does not weigh the consequences of what she does or look at the limits; her actions are reckless. Nevertheless, she confronts the military establishment and makes them uncomfortable and outraged, finds a solution to their problem, nearly pushes it through — and collapses. André Battlemont, who has been meek and mild and in love with Gwen for years, asserts himself, for the first time, when the military representatives try playing power games; he bests them by pointing out exactly what he could do to them through advertising. At this, Gwen melts — no one has ever loved her before — and the military accepts Battlemont's solution, though ungraciously. Thus there is a good deal of interest through the characterizations and the thematic elements, but much of the fun of this story comes through the confrontations between Gwen and the two generals.

All of these stories are related, to some degree, to Herbert's novels and usually explore topics, themes, and ideas that can be found in one or more of the novels. Because *Dune* is the largest and most complex of the novels, it is no surprise that most of these stories can shed light on particular elements in it. However, it is equally interesting that only one of the nineteen stories is *directly* related to one of the novels. "The Tactful Saboteur" provides the background out of which *Whipping Star* arises; this story introduces the Bureau of Sabotage and the world in which it exists at a stage approximately thirty years before the action of *Whipping Star* takes place. Furthermore, the central character in both is Jorj X. McKie, Saboteur Extraordinary, and Ser Bolin, about to begin his stint as head of the Bureau of Sabotage in the story, is very near the end of his career in the novel. Finally, the qualifications necessary for McKie to establish contact with and understanding of the Caleban in *Whipping Star* are well established in "The Tactful Saboteur." Even though the other stories do not have this kind of relationship with any given novel, the relationships they do have are illuminating.

Perhaps the thematic concern that occurs most frequently in both the novels and the stories is the nature of government, particularly as it grows larger; a prominent sub-theme concerns power-games which people play, always with a view toward expanding and preserving that power. However, Herbert does not simply repeat the same ideas over and over; instead, each of his treatments adds other elements and thus changes the theme for each story, as well as changing the overall theme that comes from an examination of all the works. All of the novels deal with this theme in some way, but it is especially a central theme in *Dune, Dune Messiah, Hellstrom's Hive,* and *The Eyes of Heisenberg.*

Almost as widespread and nearly as important as the theme of government are the closely related themes of "fools rush in" and the need to carefully adapt to the system in which one finds oneself. In many cases, the system is an ecosystem and the problem is how to use that system; furthermore, Herbert frequently makes the point that human beings as a society are a part of the ecosystem and that human society is a subsystem within the larger system. Among the novels, *Dune* and *Dune Messiah* lead the way in the exploration of these themes, stressing the length of time necessary to change the ecosystem in a sensible way; they also indicate that careful planning is necessary before such a massive change can take place. The other side of the coin, the attempt to change the ecosystem quickly, and with insufficient knowledge, is one of the main elements of *The Green Brain*. Just as the Fremen in *Dune* are closely attuned to their environment, so too are the Santarogans in *The Santaroga Barrier;* furthermore, the linkages between the individuals and the group as a whole are clear in both societies. To a lesser extent, *Hellstrom's Hive* also deals with these themes. In addition, each of the other novels seems to include an element of people acting on incomplete knowledge.

A third theme which is rather pervasive might be called "getting along with others who are different"; this includes the stories about aliens, but also includes stories about people who have different values and ways of living. For example, consider that in *Destination: Void,* an artificial intelligence is created; consider, too, the problems of learning the Freman way of life in *Dune,* trying to find out what makes the Santarogans different from the rest of the country in *The Santaroga Barrier,* the insects trying to figure out how they can contact humans to prevent destruction of the ecosystem in *The Green Brain,* the adjustment to long periods of time in a submarine in *Under Pressure,* the attempts to infiltrate the Hive in *Hellstrom's Hive,* and the exhaustive and exhausting attempts to make meaningful contact with the Caleban in *Whipping Star*—all these suggest the different directions from which Herbert explores this general theme in his novels.

There are many other themes in these stories that can be found also in the novels in a somewhat different form, although they are not used as frequently as those already mentioned. For example, the themes of heightening human awareness, the idea of racial memory, psi-powers, the limitations of prescience, and the gift/curse of unusual talents are particularly important in *Dune, Dune Messiah, The Santaroga Barrier,* and *The Godmakers.* The use of the detective story approach in "Rat Race" is particularly applicable to *The Santaroga Barrier,* while a variation on this, the spy-thriller, can be seen in both *Hellstrom's Hive* and *Under Pressure.* The emphasis on the scientific method found in such stories as "The Gone Dogs" and "By the Book" has particular relevance to *Destination: Void.* Thus, not only do these stories provide interesting, entertaining, and provocative reading in their own right, but they also complement the novels and provide a way into some of the topics explored more fully in the novels.

DUNE
1965; Nebula, Hugo Awards

For a casual reader of science fiction, reading *Dune* can be a vitalizing experience. Although there are many good science-fiction novels, none seem to have had the tremendous effect that *Dune* has had, at least on younger readers just getting into science fiction. It, probably more than any book written up to its time and more than most since, seemed to show the full promise of science fiction. It is not just that ecological matters are important now, although that helps. It is not just the idea of fighting corrupt politics, although that helps (more in 1975 than in 1965). It is not just the love story or the development of Paul's powers or the Fremen way of life or the various disciplines or the exciting sequence of events or the sense of wonder at things beyond our experience; it is not even all these things lumped together. Rather, it is the fact that Frank Herbert has created a civilization spanning many stars, in which all the factors mentioned are parts, in a consistent and coherent and comprehensive work. Few works that were written earlier even attempted *both* the breadth and the depth to be found in *Dune*.

Because *Dune* is such a rich and complex work, with such a multitude of patterns, relationships, and significances, it is impossible to hold all of them in mind at one time; perhaps the best approach is to suggest the ways in which the six basic factors which compose the literary work can be used to discover and uncover the things that are happening in the work. These six basic factors are character, story, plot, narrative point of view, setting, and language. Together, these not only provide the materials for the web of relationships that make up the book, but they also work together to create the theme (the complex of meanings that interpret experience for us) of the book. The results of an examination using these elements can be fairly brief and suggestive of further possibilities, as it will be here, or it can become quite lengthy and detailed, depending on the purposes of the person doing the analysis. In addition, these elements can be used to discover more about *any* story or book.

Probably the first aspect of the work that needs attention in a thoughtful examination is the story, the chronological-causal sequence of events. Although even this can become very complicated, what we are interested in here is the basic skeleton that holds all the rest of these elements together. For such purposes, a story event can be defined as a point at which the story makes a choice of directions, chooses one possibility rather than another. There are several ways of approaching a summary of the story. One method would provide just the bare skeleton of events and would look rather like a list or perhaps an outline.

In spite of the length of the book, the basic story-line of *Dune* is quite simple. One way of summarizing that story would be the following sequence:

1. The Atreides family moves from Caladan to Arrakis.
2. The Harkonnens attack their stronghold, killing Duke Leto.
3. Paul and Lady Jessica escape into the desert.
4. They are captured by a group of Fremen.
5. Paul fights with and kills Jamis, and as a result is accepted into the group.
6. Jessica becomes the Fremens' Reverend Mother.
7. Paul rides a gigantic sandworm, thus becoming fully initiated into the group.
8. Paul takes leadership of the Fremen.
9. The Fremen, under Paul, fight and defeat the Imperial forces.
10. Paul fights and kills Feyd-Rautha Harkonnen in formal duel.
11. Paul deposes the Emperor.

Each of these marks a point at which the story could go one of several directions, and each of them follows logically from, is "caused" by, what has gone before. It might be noted, too, that these also summarize a large number of specific actions. Furthermore, different people may very well add different elements to this list, or phrase them differently, for, in part at least, this is a matter of the point of view from which the actions of the book are seen; the reasoning behind the choices is as important as the choices themselves. Finally, more specific story events link each of these major events; for example, under number 3 (Paul and Jessica escape into the desert), you would have such specific actions, in sequence, as their initial capture, being taken to the desert to be left helpless, escaping their guards, help from a group of Fremen led by Liet Kynes, flight in an ornithopter through a desert storm, and the walk across the desert. These specific steps lead from number 3 directly to number 4. However, even without considering these specific steps or the details of the Harkonnen plotting which moves beside this story-line, this outline can suggest several things about the thematic content of the novel. First of all, these events show Paul's rise from the son of a murdered duke to the ruler of the Empire; certainly the political maneuvering involved in the novel will yield materials for a theme. At the same time that this rise is taking place, Paul also moves from a familiar place to a strange one, learning the ways of the strange situation and gradually, through a series of steps, becoming a member of a new group and finally a leader of that group; thematically, this suggests two directions: the learning process and the nature of the group he is becoming a part of. Thus, even if one did no more than outline the major actions that take place in the book and think about them for a time, some of the areas which the fully fleshed-out novel provides an interpretation for can be seen. Naturally, if the specifics of those interpretations are to be found, we must go to other elements of the novel to find them.

A second way of summarizing the story's events is to take a more narrative stance, providing more information about relationships, motivations, and points of thematic stress. While the first method makes it somewhat easier to see the main outlines of the short story or novel as a framework to which other elements have been added, the second approach makes it somewhat easier to move directly into a discussion of the thematic elements of the work. Nevertheless, both approaches cover basically the same events and the same materials. For example, a summary of the story using the second approach would be something like this:

In its main outlines, the story-line emphasizes the political struggle and the development of Paul Atreides. It begins in political maneuvering, for the Atreides family has been requested (ordered politely but without honorable alternative) by the Emperor to leave the planet Caladan, their ducal fief for many generations, to take over the governance of Arrakis from the Harkonnens, who are long-time enemies, and to supervise the gathering of melange. Both the Harkonnens and the Emperor have reason to want to put Duke Leto Atreides in a more vulnerable position so they can destroy him. The active role in this partnership is taken by Baron Vladimir Harkonnen, who has planted a traitor in the Atreides household and who has followers on Arrakis. Thus, before the Duke and his family can get fully settled in and well-defended, Harkonnen forces, including the Imperial Sardaukar in Harkonnen uniforms, storm the castle. They kill many, Leto dying as he tries to poison Baron Harkonnen, others are captured, notably Thufir Hawat, and a few escape, notably Gurney Halleck. Paul and his mother, the Lady Jessica, are temporarily captive but use their training to escape. Dr. Yueh, the traitor who hates what he does, has provided a survival kit and sent them toward protection; he also sent the Atreides ducal signet, so that Paul may have proof of his ancestry when he needs it. The Fremen, natives of the planet, under Kynes, the planetary ecologist who has given them a vision of the future, help them escape further and give them an ornithopter. They escape pursuit in a sandstorm, though the plane eventually fails them. After crossing the desert on foot, they are captured by another group of Fremen; although their leader would tentatively accept them, one of his men would kill them immediately, in observance of the traditions of the tribe. Eventually, Paul must fight with this man, Jamis; he does so and kills him in formal combat. This wins his acceptance by the tribe and earns him the familiar and formal Fremen names of Usul and Muad'Dib. Shortly thereafter, Jessica becomes Reverend

Mother to the Fremen. As he lives with the Fremen, Paul grows in the Fremen ways, leading up to the test of riding the Maker, a giant sandworm of Arrakis. After he has done so, he rapidly acquires a leadership role among the Fremen and leads them on greater raids against the Harkonnen, who have repossessed the planet. Paul also drinks the Water of Life, a poison used in creating the Reverend Mothers, who have the ability to transmute it; he survives it and it brings his powers into full being. Finally, the need to combat these raids, as well as various political motives, bring the Harkonnen and Imperial forces in great strength to Arrakis. With the aid of a storm, the family atomics, and riding the Makers, the Fremen led by Paul overcome the numerically superior forces arrayed against them. After formal combat with Feyd-Rautha Harkonnen, whom he kills, Paul deposes the Emperor, taking his daughter as wife, though vowing she will be his wife in name only. Thus, Paul's revenge for the death of his father is completed, and the novel ends.

This second approach to summarizing the story may lead slightly more easily into the next aspect of the novel that, especially for *Dune*, might most profitably be looked at. This aspect would be character, that bundle of qualities and traits that individuals in the novel are composed of, and the relationships between characters. Since any reading of the novel, as well as the two kinds of story summary, indicate that Paul Atreides is the central character in the novel, he should be the starting point. Paul's characteristics are many and varied, for comparatively speaking he is quite well-rounded. He has exceptional powers of observation and bodily control, having been trained in the Bene Gesserit way. His powers of logic and deduction are above normal, having been trained as a Mentat. He has a keen sense of the uses and intricacies of power and political maneuvering, having been raised as the son of a duke who will one day take over his father's position. He is intelligent and thus able to use these different kinds of training well. He has a gift of foretelling. He develops into the Kwisatz Haderach because of his genetic heritage, the necessities of life on Arrakis, the pressure of revenge for his father, and his training. Revenge is a strong motivating factor in many of his actions, particularly those dealing with the Emperor and the Harkonnens. He is also capable of love, though not for many people; he is loyal to those who look to him for leadership. Paul also has many other traits and many relationships with other characters in the novel. There are also many other characters, and the entire web of relationships is immense and complex. Those characteristics which have been indicated, however, can serve to show how story and character interact to clarify a thematic position. One of the thematic areas suggested by the storyline is the learning process that Paul undergoes; the specifics of his character indicate the nature, the direction, and some of the means to achieve this learning. In the novel itself we are shown some of Paul's training in weapons, in thinking, in the use of physical control, and in practical govern-ment; for the most part, however, this kind of training is in the background, something that has already taken place. Instead, in the interaction between the events and his character, we see Paul gradually learning how to bring these various skills together, to understand their nature so that he can apply them to the specific problem of avenging his father and leading the Fremen to a position where they can safely work toward their goal of a green planet. As he learns to control these abilities, he also comes to understand more about himself and his place in the specific situation and in history. To a certain extent, his survival makes it necessary for him to learn these things, so the setting will also be important to the learning process; his abilities, plus his interaction with the Fremen and with the setting, as well as the desire for revenge, all come together to provide the means by which he finds the resources for growth. Through the course of the novel, he grows in several directions: in understanding himself, in his ability to control his abilities to achieve a desired end, in his ability to lead others, in his knowledge of the world around him, and in his ability to see himself as part of a much larger context. All of these things furnish further details for a thematic statement dealing with the learning process Paul undergoes. Other aspects of his character and of his relationships with other char-acters add depth, breadth, and detail to other thematic possibilities.

Although the other characters are given sufficient characterization so that we can assume that they have a separate life of their own, they are primarily important because of their relationships with Paul. The Lady Jessica, for example, is a Bene Gesserit, which implies a number of things about her training, her abilities, and her purposes; the first two of these are shown through the action in various situations, as well as being implied by what we see of other Bene Gesserits in the novel, but the third is im-plied through the actions of Reverend Mother Gaius Helen Mohiam and of Lady Fenring and through the general background about the Bene Gesserit that is provided throughout the novel. In addition, she is the con-cubine of Duke Leto, which implies that she has certain duties within his household and a set of feelings related to him; some of the specifics which define these are provided, and, from them, the reader can imagine others. Finally, she becomes a Reverend Mother for the Fremen, which means that she again has duties in that connection, although these are left gen-erally vague. Thus, although in many ways she is defined in relationship to others, we can imagine her as leading a life outside of her relationship to Paul. Nevertheless, it is that relationship that gives her place and im-portance in the novel; these other elements also focus on the relationship she has with her son. For example, her Bene Gesserit training allows her to pass this on to Paul, providing one of the elements that make him what he is; that training in tandem with her feeling for Duke Leto enables her

story, the novel's treatment of political power and political maneuvering is one of the points that Herbert has treated rather consistently, though with various points of view and specific materials, throughout his works. At first glance, it seems that the saying "power corrupts; absolute power corrupts absolutely," might be an adequate summation of his theme. It becomes quite clear, for example, that the main reason that the Emperor is willing to help the Baron Harkonnen destroy the House of Atreides is that he feels a threat from both of these men; since Leto is the more capable of the two men, he is to be destroyed; also, he can use this destruction as a threat against the Baron to hold him in check. In short, the Emperor is using his power to preserve that power and to preserve the flow of money from the spice. In addition to this, when it comes to a showdown on Arrakis, the Emperor is most concerned with the court functions that he will have to miss and with the threat to the flow of spice; he does not really think in terms of human beings at all: it doesn't really bother him that only one of the five troop carriers that he sent to the south returned, but he is bothered by the fact that it was old men, women, and children who inflicted this defeat, for this may mean that his power is more threatened than he thought it to be earlier. Baron Harkonnen is also corrupt and a user of men for his own ends. In a sense, he is even more dangerous than the Emperor, for while the Emperor has all the power available, the Baron would like more than he has, and he is willing to use any means that he can to attain that power. Furthermore, both of these men are exploitors, concerned with taking as much from Arrakis as they can, and as quickly as they can. They have no concern about depleting the planet, and as little concern about the men and equipment who do the actual work of getting the spice. It does seem that these two men, and those surrounding them, do indeed fit that quotation. However, opposed to these two we find two other leaders who do not quite fit into that mold. Duke Leto Atreides, for example, is much more concerned about men than about either machines or the spice if a choice must be made between them; some of his plans for Arrakis include ways of making the spice gathering safer, and he does risk his own life to save the lives of men in a spice factory when they are threatened by a sandworm. He also aims to lead by example rather than by fear, by uniting rather than by polarizing. He is not perfect, of course, but he strives to keep the human above the abstract. He is well aware of the power that is to be gained by building a fighting force equal to that of the Emperor, but he seems to be more interested in using it to preserve a balance than in gaining power for himself. Perhaps his most serious breach of this ideal is when he tells himself that Kynes will have to learn how to speak properly to him. Another example of a good leader who is little corrupted by the power that he has is Stilgar, the leader of the Fremen. He impresses Jessica immediately with his knowledge of his men, with his way of trying to persuade them from actions he does not approve of, with his bowing to the voice of the tribe, and with his understanding of many things, including the necessity of change. Furthermore, in all his actions he keeps the welfare of his tribe as his topmost concern; he is even willing to allow himself to be killed if this will help them in the future. Though he will fight for his power, it is not for the same reason that the Emperor fights for his; Stilgar will fight in order to ensure that the challenger is fit to take his place as the leader and protector of his people, not simply to keep the power for himself, as can be seen when the young men of the tribe are suggesting that Paul should be their leader. Though both of these men may not be perfect leaders, they cannot be said to have been corrupted by their power. The real center of this theme, however, is Paul Muad'Dib, the Atreides Duke and the leader of the Fremen. By the time the novel ends, he has greater power than any man has had before, and he must find a way to control it. It is not just that he has power over the Fremen, nor that he takes over the Imperial throne, but rather that, with his awareness of the future and the sense of purpose that has been bred into him, both strengthened by his experiences, he represents a turning point in human history, a point which he must try to manage in the best possible way and with the least possible damage to mankind as a whole. This is a great burden, and the only person who can sense what he must do is Alia. Nevertheless, Paul does seem to manage to resist the corruptions of power quite well, for he sorrows when he sees Stilgar become a worshipper; he is willing to make the Emperor as comfortable as possible on the prison planet; he feels great tenderness for Chani; and he still shares the Fremen dream of a green planet. However, he is also a realist, and does those things which must be done directly and without thought about who may be hurt. He has the realization that any choice is not between good and bad alternatives, but rather that making any choice may hurt someone; he has chosen the jihad, with the Fremen running wild over the worlds of the Imperium, for he has seen that the other main direction of the future is even worse, even less desirable. Furthermore, he has seen that he has really never had the choice of preventing either of them; all he can do is try to minimize the unpleasant consequences. The choices facing Paul are very complex; in judging him, we cannot make simple judgments, but rather must take into consideration the situations and the possibilities facing him. Whatever decision is made, it can be nothing as simple as "power corrupts; absolute power corrupts absolutely."

Although the ecological theme is not the most visible or the most directly developed theme in the novel, there is reason to think that it contains the idea which gave impetus to writing this novel. Basically speaking, this theme consists of several elements: the nature and balance of the planet as it is at the time of the story; the ways that people have adapted to those conditions, both those who live with them and those who fight against them; and the vision of a green planet, including the ecologically sound plan for gradually bringing this vision into reality. Each of these elements is complex in itself, and only a few basic points can be examined here. Obviously, the main fact about this planet is that it is almost completely desert, with only very small polar ice caps. Just as clearly, water is a matter of greatest concern, especially among those who have neither the funds nor the connections to have water shipped to them from other worlds. It is implied that there is sufficient water on the planet to make a change in these conditions, although finding it in a usable form is very difficult. At the very least, extremely careful planning and very sophisticated means of gathering this water are needed if any such effort in that direction is to be successful. And, of course, a great deal of care is needed in order to preserve the life that is already there. The Fremen were not originally natives of Arrakis, having been brought there as slaves; however, they have adapted themselves and their entire life styles to the planet and to the desire to survive. It is noteworthy, for example, that they are capable of rather sophisticated technology, but that all their efforts are concentrated on things related to preserving water. Their burial customs, their treatment of strangers, their mode of travel (both walking and on wormback), their soitches, and their stillsuits—all of these things are directly related to the conditions which they face and to ensuring the survival of the tribe. Their vision of the future of the planet seems based on two things: their memory of the world they came from which they keep alive through ritual, and the word of Kynes about how they can make this world a green one. Patience is a survival trait on this planet, so they are ideally suited to the long period of time that is necessary for this plan to work. Kynes, then, provides the basic plan, the means of bringing about a change in an ecologically sound manner so that needed forms of life can either adapt to the changing conditions or be replaced by other life forms which can serve a similar function in the changed environment; the Fremen supply the devotion to the cause and the particular application of the plans that will make this dream a reality. Both Kynes and the Fremen, as well as Paul and Jessica, realize, however, that the change cannot be complete, for the thing which makes the planet important is the spice, and water is poison for the sandworms who produce the spice in their earliest forms. In addition, Paul values the strength of body and mind that are found among the Fremen, and recognizes that in large measure these are a result of the type of life that they have lived; he would also like to see that there are at least spots on Arrakis where their original way of life can be returned to, no matter what other changes are introduced. It might be noted that everything that is said in this novel about changing the planet is ecologically sound and scientifically feasible; the only questionable area is the source of the water that will be needed to start this cycle in any significant way, but this is something that is not gone into at any length and there are suggestions that the planet does have the sources, so that we can accept this without undue strain to our credibility. In a very basic sense, then, these factors which constitute the ecological theme of the novel are responsible for much that happens in this novel.

When dealing with science fiction, there is another point that can profitably be examined, whether before or after the sort of analysis suggested. Since many, though not all, science fiction stories and novels seem to have begun with the writer's speculation about "what would happen if . . . ," it is reasonable to try to determine what the core question of the work might be—that is, what question seems to give rise to the largest number of the specific factors in the novel? In the case of *Dune*, this core question seems to be something like this: what would happen if there were a desert planet that was the source of a valuable natural resource? The fact that it had a valuable resource would account for the interest in it and probably also for the fact that it is inhabited. The fact that it is a desert would account for the native social structure, the planet's ecology, and the difficulties posed for those who would exploit the resources. The properties of the spice account for its value to a divergent group of customers; that value, in turn, gives impetus to exploitation and the political maneuvering that accompanies the desire to gain the profits. As mentioned before, the political system found in the novel is at least one logical answer to this situation. Since a desert planet is not generally habitable, and cannot directly support more than a very few people, the existence of other settled planets is reasonable. If there are other planets, and travel between them, it is to be expected that the natives of Arrakis would have heard of green worlds, and that they would be envious of an ideal that would be the opposite of their everyday existence, especially if there were someone to lead them. To have hopes for achieving that goal, an unusual political leader would be necessary; the specific things which would make him unusual would not be specified by this requirement, but Paul's character is certainly adequate. It may be true that not everything can be tied, directly or indirectly, back to this core question, but as it is stated it does provide a way of getting into an extremely large number of specific aspects of the novel; the points that have been mentioned are only the beginning. The main benefit of the core question is that it provides something quite specific to center thinking and discussion around, a point to which one can return and to which one can relate other points. It may also point toward themes or toward areas that a reader might be interested in speculating about himself. More important, though, it can provide a starting point for examining the work and a direction from which to work; it is especially valuable for science fiction because of the speculative nature of the field.

Dune, which is extremely rich in materials and in ideas, not only points toward future possibilities but also has relevance for mankind here and now. Not only is there a breadth and sweep to this novel, but there is also a good deal of depth to many of the ideas that it explores; it is a coherent novel which is nevertheless complex. Because of these things, there will be very few who will disagree with the idea that *Dune* is, at the very least, one of the five or ten best science-fiction novels that have yet been written — if it isn't the best.

DUNE MESSIAH
1969

Dune Messiah picks up the story begun in *Dune* some twelve years after Paul conquered the Emperor's forces and took the reins of power. During that time, the Jihad power, foreseen and dreaded by Paul, began and spread from world to world; by the time *Dune Messiah* opens, it still continues, though it is in its dying moments. Several results are quite important to the novel; however, in terms of the over-all background, the one which may be most important — the mingling and revitalization of the gene pool throughout the Empire — is mentioned but not stressed. One result that does play an important role in this novel, of course, is the spread of a religion centered around Paul and, to a lesser extent, Alia; another is a general solidification of Paul's position as Emperor. Negatively, there exists the destruction done to the Fremen way of life and to individual Fremen. Finally, there are a number of rebellions and conspiracies against Paul, engendered by his power, his cult, and the means by which they were attained and solidified; the most prominent of these is, quite naturally, the one involving the Princess Irulan, the Reverend Mother Gaius Helen Mohiam, Edric of the Space Guild, and Scytale of the Tleilaxu Face Dancers; between them they represent most of the powerful elements in the old Empire. It is on these results of the Jihad which much of the action and interest of *Dune Messiah* centers.

The story in *Dune Messiah* is more scattered, less simple, and less action-oriented than that in *Dune*. Whereas in the first novel, although things happened to Paul and shaped him, he was nevertheless an active force who had a direct part in shaping the action and its direction; in this second novel, he seems to be playing a waiting game, allowing a number of factors to mature and come together before acting to bring about a foreseen culmination. Thus, a summary of events might be outlined in this way:
Representatives of the Space Guild (Edric), the Bene Gesserit (Reverend Mother Gaius Helen Mohiam), the Bene Tleilaxu (Scytale), and the Emperor's household (Princess Irulan) meet to plot against Paul Muad'dib.
Chani tries to convince Paul to produce an heir with Irulan, since she has not conceived again; Paul recalls a conversation earlier that day with

Irulan on that same subject.

Scytale visits Farok to gain information; before he leaves, he kills Farok and his son.

At a council meeting, Paul decides to sign a treaty giving refuge to Great Houses in hiding and to accept an ambassador from the Space Guild.

The Space Guild ambassador (Edric) is presented at court; he presents Paul with a Bene Tleilaxu ghola with the features of Duncan Idaho.

Paul has the Reverend Mother Gaius Helen Mohiam arrested from the Guild heighliner which brought Edric to Arrakis.

Irulan visits the Reverend Mother in her cell.

Edric again visits Paul.

Alia and the ghola view a dead body to find clues as to who it was and who killed her and to talk at length during their return.

Paul has a dream of a falling moon, which he discusses with the ghola.

The Reverend Mother is brought before Paul, so that he might bargain with her for Chani's life, offering artificial insemination of Irulan in exchange (a long forbidden thing).

Scytale visits Edric to arrange the next step in their plot.

Paul is summoned to Otheym's by Scytale in the guise of Otheym's daughter so that he might be given information about conspirators.

Paul walks through the city alone to meet his guide, watching the Evening Rite at Alia's Fane on the way; he meets the guide, who takes him the rest of the way.

Otheym informs him of treachery and sends the dwarf Bijaz, who has been imprinted (mentally) with names, etc.; he waits to leave until his vision of the moment is completed in reality.

As Paul had foreseen, a stone burner destroys Otheym's house, blinds Paul and others, and kills still others; he continues acting through his knowledge from his visions.

Alia presides over the trial of Korba, the head of the Qizarate (the religious arm of the Empire), for conspiracy, including the stealing of a sandworm and the use of the stone burner.

Hayt (the ghola) and Bijaz confront one another, Bijaz "keying" Hayt for the job he was made to do.

Hayt prevents Alia's death from an overdose of melange.

Paul takes Chani and a large company of others to the desert, to Sietch Tabr.

Chani dies giving birth to twins.

Paul, by his actions, forces Hayt/Duncan Idaho to break through to reclaim his past as Idaho.

The moment when Paul's vision ends arrives, and he is left totally blind.

Scytale comes into the room of birth to force Paul to bargain with him.

Paul's son—just born—links with him telepathically, revealing to him the whole male line at the same time, and lends him his eyes.

With this borrowed vision, Paul kills Scytale by throwing a crysknife. Following Fremen tradition, Paul walks alone into the desert.

This sequence of events is not as simple and straightforward as the sequence in *Dune;* in fact, although these events do appear in this order in the novel and although they seem to follow one another chronologically, they seem to lack the kind of causal relationship that would make them a true story-sequence. In a sense, these events seem leading, for the most part, toward Paul's death through the machinations of the conspirators introduced in the first section of the novel. However, the fact that Paul walks alone into the desert after killing Scytale indicates that the conspirators have failed, a failure which goes beyond not killing him, and that, therefore, this chronology must have other purposes than the apparent one. To look at these means moving from action and events into the areas of character and theme, into the details with which these events are filled out. Thus, from Paul's perspective, these events represent bringing the forces with which his empire and his religion—and he, himself—must contend into an alignment which will permit a culmination of his career that will also consolidate what he has gained and change the direction of history. In this sense, the most important event in the novel, the event toward which Paul has been aiming, is not his death but rather the birth of his children. The significance of this will be discussed in more detail in the following section, for it has much to do with the unity and continuity of *Dune* and *Dune Messiah* and may suggest the direction which the third volume of the series, now being written, will take.

As the story summary indicates quite clearly, the major thematic concern of the novel lies in the political sphere. But while the story line emphasizes the political conspiracy against Paul, the novel as a whole brings many other elements to bear in its exploration of this theme. One of these elements, which is barely suggested in the story summary, involves the changes in the Fremen way of life brought about by the Jihad and by following Paul as their leader. One of the first of these results that is noticeable is the fact that many of the Fremen that we see are crippled in some way: Farok has lost an arm; his son is blind; Otheym's daughter is a semuta addict; Otheym himself caught the splitting disease on Tarahell; in fact, the entire area of the city in which they live is composed of veterans of the Jihad, most of whom seem to be scarred in some way. Perhaps even more important than the physical scars, however, are the mental scars some of them carry. Farok is the primary example of this, although it is clear that he is not alone. He speaks of the nobility of his people in the past tense, feeling that now they have been degraded and cast out. He is bitter that his son has lost his eyes and that, consequently, no Fremen woman will have him. He is bitter about the number of the dead and maimed, blaming Muad'dib and doubting that he knows or cares about the number. He feels that the companionship and the closeness of mind and spirit of the sietch have been lost. He is bitter about his poverty, even though he admits that it represents wealth he could not at one time even imagine; he feels he has lost the true wealth that was his in the sietch. He has been changed by his experiences in profound ways, one of the most important of which can be seen by the way that he holds his door open when Scytale arrives, allowing the moisture within to escape; the rapidity with which Paul is greening Arrakis and the overwhelming amounts of water seen on other planets have destroyed the vision and one of the basic values which held the Fremen society together before the influence of the Jihad. Because of all these things, he is willing to enter into a conspiracy against the Emperor, who was also a sietch mate, and to forsake the ties of the sietch; this extends even to helping smuggle a sandworm off Arrakis in an attempt to break Paul's monopoly, an act that would earlier have been totally unthinkable. Farok, of course, is not the only Fremen who is unsatisfied, but rather is a representative of many, for the conspiracy is spread throughout Fremen society and beyond it; consider, here, Irulan's statement that many are looking backward with longing toward her father's reign. In addition to these factors, the Fremen Naibs have, for the most part, gone soft. They seem to feel that they have been displaced in their positions of leadership among their people and, thus, lost. Some of them, of course, like Farok, have become a part of the conspiracy. Most of those who have not entered into it seem only to sit back and allow things to happen, without taking any leadership responsibilities. By the end of the novel, most of those involved in the conspiracy have been uncovered and dealt with. It is toward the remaining Fremen that Paul's final gesture is aimed: by walking alone into the desert to give his water to Shai-hulud, he reaffirms the Fremen tradition and his bond with it, thus also reminding the Fremen of the way that gave them strength and purpose, as well as insuring their loyalty.

The motives of the others who are involved in the reaction against Paul's empire are extremely mixed. Irulan, for example, becomes involved because she wishes to bear the child of the kwisatz haderach and because she feels the actions against her father quite strongly, although this is by far the lessor of the two forces motivating her. Even her desire to bear Paul's child is a complex desire: she wants it because it would proclaim her place and remove the slight of being a wife in name only, because she is a Bene Gesserit who has been ordered to preserve the bloodline in a controlled way, because she would thus be able to be a formative figure in founding a new political dynasty, and, if her "conversion" at the end of the novel is any true indication, because she loves and admires Paul. Naturally enough, it is this child that the other conspirators offer her to bring her into the fold. The Space Guild, represented by Edric, obviously resents the control placed on them by Paul's ability to destroy the spice; after all, before Paul came to power, the Guild could dictate *its* terms in any situation because they had a monopoly on travel between planets, as well as other devices, whereas Paul can now dictate *his* terms to *them* because he controls the spice they need so badly, not only for navigation but also for life itself. While Irulan represents a link with Paul's household, Edric's contribution to the conspiracy is the inability of one prescient to "see" another through his visions, thus hiding their meetings and many of their other activities. In a sense, vengeance and loss of power are also the motivations of the Bene Gesserit and especially of the Reverend Mother Gaius Helen Mohiam. Whereas they had previously been able to control the directions of the Empire and of the individual Great Houses, now they have been discredited and have no foothold in the Empire. They also resent Paul and Alia, at least partly because they cannot control them, although Reverend Mother Mohiam's failure to admit the possibilities of Paul's being the kwisatz haderach contributed heavily to this situation. In addition, they are trying to regain some measure of control through the children — that is, if Irulan bears a child of Paul's, then the breeding line will be known and, through her, they can direct the child; although they hesitate at artificial insemination, they seem to consider the possibility of using a Tleilaxu ghola of Paul for this purpose. In fact, should it become possible/ necessary to use gholas, they seem interested in mating Paul with Alia to see what would result.

The motives of the Bene Tleilaxu are much more obscure than those of any other group reacting against the Empire of Paul Muad'dib. Mentioned only briefly in *Dune,* and their function never clearly delineated in either novel, they seem to be a guild of scientists, whose science cuts across the boundaries of what we call the hard and the soft sciences. For example, they have produced artificial eyes, have perfected the technique of regrowing bodies from cells of the original (that is, in making a ghola such as that of Hayt/Duncan Idaho), and have worked in controlled and accelerated mutation to the point where they developed their own kwisatz haderach. However, in addition to these achievements in the hard sciences, they also seem to be particularly interested in psychology, for one of the reasons that they developed their kwisatz haderach was, apparently, to study his reactions and psychological processes; their interest in and manipulation of the ghola of Duncan Idaho reveals both an extensive knowledge of the human mind and a desire to know more. Their Face Dancers seem to have been another biological experiment which was turned into an excellent tool for the intrigues which seem to have been rampant throughout both the old and the new Empires. Their role in the conspiracy seems to be largely that of an interested observer, using an opportunity to gain further knowledge of human psychology and of political systems in practice; whereas the other members of the group of four have something against Paul personally, only Scytale indicates compassion for him and some regret at what he is about to do. Not only is the Face Dancer an excellent tool, for he can enter many places unknown, but also he seems to be the prime mover of the entire plot; this point is not stressed, but it seemes quite clear in our first introduction to him.

Although they have no representation in the meeting which opens the novel, the Qizarate, the priesthood of the religion focused around Paul, is also heavily involved in the conspiracy, as well as being responsible for a fair share of the unrest in the Empire. They are not so much against Paul as they are for gaining power for themselves; this is particularly true of Korba, the Panegyrist and a member of Paul's Council. It is certainly not that they have lacked power; indeed, since Paul's reign began, they have steadily increased their power as the Jihad spread the new religion from world to world. In addition, however, the religious and political arms of the Empire are inextricably interwoven. Not only is the Qizarate Panegyrist on the highest Council of the Empire, but by far the largest portion of the "civil service" jobs are filled by members of the religious order. Furthermore, the priesthood also serves as a spy system, presumably to inform the Emperor, but also to give information to the religious hierarchy. Apparently, having tasted power and seeing it increase rapidly, Korba and others close to him have acquired a desire for more. Another factor underlying the Qizarate's involvement in the conspiracy seems to be the fact that Paul rather firmly limits what they can do in, and with, his name. Both he and Alia (who is the high priestess), for example, mock Korba's pomposity about leading the pilgrims in prayer and his attempts to cast a religious coating over his spy system. Both ignore his advice and have as little as possible to do with religious duties; in this latter area, Alia must bear a greater portion of service than Paul, and she dislikes it intensely. Since the Qizarate, and Korba particularly, take themselves and their mission exceedingly seriously, these attitudes disturb them a great deal.

Thus, a large portion of the book is devoted to portraying the various stages and methods which these groups use to maneuver Paul into a position where they think he will be vulnerable and likely to satisfy their desires. Although Paul does not seem to be particularly concerned about the various facets of this conspiracy, many of his actions, direct and indirect, suggest that he is much more aware of them than his opponents seem to believe. For example, although he cannot "see" the actions of a Space Guildsman through his prescience, he can tell where one has been and what possible directions he will go. Although, because of the Guildsman's cover, he cannot tell exactly what Irulan was doing on her trip to Wallach, both he and Chani know positively that secret decisions were made during it. Twice, Paul is able to penetrate the disguise of the Face Dancer. Even before he goes to Otheym's house, he is aware that he will be blinded. He apparently knows why Chani has not conceived, for she does as soon as a new diet is ordered for her. And he carefully brings the major conspirators along into the desert when Chani is to give birth. Not only is he aware of such details as these but he is also aware of the pattern, or the multitude of possible patterns, of which they are only parts. While there are limitations on Paul's prescient powers—he cannot "see" where Tuptile is, he expects Chani to bear him only one child, and he had not foreseen Bijaz when he visits Otheym's—it is clear that he has chosen one of the patterns that the future could take and is following that pattern as closely as he possibly can, down to the point of not leaving Otheym's until the proper words have been spoken. His success in following this pattern can be measured by his exact descriptions of the scene after the explosion or at the beginning of Korba's trial.

There are a number of significant factors in his choice of this pattern of events which he is following so carefully. As early as the first indications in *Dune* of the role he is to play among the Fremen, Paul wishes that he could simply back out of the situation into which he has been thrust. However, he also realizes that this is not one of the real choices, that his entrance into the world of Arrakis has set in motion certain forces that not even his death could halt. His final decision to lead the Fremen against the Harkonnen and the Emperor and on into the Jihad, while the results would be shattering, is due to his vision that this is the least of the possible evils, that even greater destruction would follow from any of the other possible courses he might take. Nevertheless, though he is ruthless and direct when the need arises, he is fully aware of the destructiveness of his reign; he does not like what he must do, nor does he like what is being done in his name. Thus, since his early involvement with the Fremen, one of his strongest motivations seems to have been finding the best possible moment to withdraw from the situation, with death his only means of doing so. At the same time, however, he is also aware that his reign marks a turning point in human history. Although it is not clearly specified, it seems probable that this turn might be good, bad, or indifferent, depending on how various situations turn out. Another element which is not specified—it will probably be the basic subject of the third novel in the sequence—is the path which Paul would like to insure that the Empire will follow. It would seem, though, that the most important step in establishing this path is the birth of an heir, a child of Chani's. It also seems important that the Bene Gesserit, the Bene Tleilaxu, the Space Guild, and the Qizarate be rather firmly discredited and to lose some of their power and sureness of themselves. It is necessary also that the power and belief of the Fremen be cemented into loyalty to the House of Atreides, so that they will support Paul's heirs. Finally, it is necessary for Paul to die when these things have been accomplished, or to accomplish them in dying. It is probable, of course, that his death in the Fremen way will not only firmly establish Fremen loyalty, but also, through the religion, cement the loyalty and belief of many others. Given these factors and these desired results, much of the political action of the novel can be seen as maneuverings to bring these things to pass.

There are several other elements related to government interspersed throughout the novel. There are also the rather thematic threads of religion and of Paul's development, which are quite prominent in *Dune Messiah.* However, since these things seem to have a direct bearing on the unity and continuity of *Dune* and *Dune Messiah,* they will be discussed in some detail in the following section of this study.

THE UNIT AND CONTINUITY OF *DUNE* AND *DUNE MESSIAH*

Many readers of science fiction were disappointed by *Dune Messiah;* they felt that it does not, somehow, live up to the expectations created by *Dune.* There is also some feeling that the two novels are not parts of a unified whole and that a sense of continuity, though present, falters. While it is true that *Dune Messiah* has a narrower focus than *Dune* and that our understanding of much of what happens in the sequel is dependent upon the mass of detail provided in the earlier novel, consequently leaving *Dune Messiah* less rich and complex in its own right, nevertheless the two novels belong together and must be viewed as two segments of a larger whole. Perhaps the clearest and most fruitful way of viewing the unity and the continuity of the two novels is to look at them as a sophisticated form of Heroic Romance.

The central feature of Heroic Romance is the quest of the hero. In outline, this quest is quite simple: something causes the hero to set forth on his quest; as he proceeds, he must overcome a series of obstacles or tests; having successfully overcome them, he goes after the object of his quest; if he is successful in achieving it, the king's daughter and at least a portion of the kingdom are his normal rewards. However, this central feature of Heroic Romance is normally preceded by the advent and initiation of the hero and often is followed by the apotheosis—the transcendence of the human condition—of the hero. Thus, in the advent and initiation phase of Heroic Romance, the hero is born (often accompanied by unusual signs or situations), he passes some preliminary trials, and he is initiated into the heroic condition. In the last phase, his heroic status is affirmed, he consolidates what he has gained, and he dies, though his death establishes his godlikeness. Because many of the traditional forms of Heroic Romance end with the hero's achievement and reward, which does provide a sense of completion and closure, *Dune* seems to be complete in itself. Nevertheless, the apotheosis of the hero is a natural and inevitable—though not always specified—conclusion to Heroic Romance; it is this phase of the hero's life that *Dune Messiah* provides.

Like the last phase, the first phase of Heroic Romance assumes a world without the hero, though the hero's advent may have been expected or prepared for before his actual birth. In addition to the hero's birth, this first phase of advent and initiation establishes the hero's credentials and his initiation into the heroic condition, which is often done in the form of some kind of preliminary test he must pass. All of these elements are present in *Dune,* although only the preliminary test is shown directly. Paul's birth has been prepared for and not prepared for—that is, Paul is in the prime breeding line that the Bene Gesserit have created in their attempts to develop a kwisatz haderach, a male Bene Gesserit whose powers of mind would go beyond theirs to penetrate hidden areas of the psyche and to bridge space and time; however, the Bene Gesserit were not prepared for the disobedience of the Lady Jessica in producing a son rather than the daughter she had been ordered to bear, nor were they ready to believe that this son might actually be the kwisatz haderach. Nevertheless, they did apply the preliminary test to Paul Atreides. Furthermore, he passed the test of the gom jabbar, a test requiring physical and mental control while undergoing great pain; in doing so, he withstood greater pain with greater control than anyone tested before him. Even in the face of this evidence, the Reverend Mother Gaius Helen Mohiam is unwilling to accept him as a potential kwisatz haderach; for the reader, however, this establishes Paul's heroic condition.

Paul also has other credentials that mark him as a potential hero. It might be remembered here that frequently the hero is an embodiment of the highest ideals of the society in which he exists, though he may also point beyond them. Thus, his birth to Duke Leto Atreides and his legal concubine establishes his royal blood and his right to rule in a hierarchical society. As befits a ducal heir, Paul has also been trained in the ways of leadership and in the ways of battle. Although it might be expected that a Duke would provide the best training possible for his heir, it is significant that Paul's instructors are among the very best in the entire society; that is, Leto himself is reputed to be one of the best-loved and effective planetary rulers in the system, and both Gurney Halleck and Duncan Idaho rank very high among those involved in forms of combat and tactics. This training might in itself be sufficient to establish Paul's heroic credentials. However, Lady Jessica has disobeyed her superiors on a second matter, for she has undertaken to train her *son* (only daughters were to be so trained, for only they were eligible to become Bene Gesserit before the appearance of the kwisatz haderach) in the Bene Gesserit ways of physical and mental discipline; her success can be seen in Paul's reaction to the gom jabbar. It is implied that a very few other males—all potential Kwisatz Haderachs who did not quite reach the level of genetic perfection required—have received similar training, thus making Paul a member of a very small company. However, a third facet of his training makes Paul unique in his society and in human history; that is, his training as a Mentat Assassin, itself a rather restricted combination, at the hands of Thufir Hawat, Leto's Mentat Assassin. All of these ways in which Paul is trained are either necessities or ideals of his society. None of them are unique or unusual in the society. Rather, what makes Paul unique is the combination of the ways in which he has been trained; never before has the son of a duke been trained as a Mentat, much less as a Mentat Assassin, *and* in the Bene Gesserit way. Of course, no birth and no amount of training are of any value unless the hero can put all his potentials together and realize them in action. The main function of the preliminary test is to suggest that the hero will be able to do so, a test which Paul passes in a way superior to expectations. This test also provides two further elements: Paul is given a lesson in political expedience by the Reverend Mother, and he gives evidence of his prescient vision. Thus, his credentials as a potential hero are clearly established and several fore-shadowings of the future are suggested early in the novel.

The move from Caladan to Arrakis creates the preliminary conditions for the quest by moving Paul from a stable, secure environment into a situation which is both unstable and insecure. The attack by the Harkonnen forces and the concommitant death of Duke Leto, of course, provide the specific motivation for Paul's quest, but before this takes place, some necessary groundwork for future events is laid. The most important of these involves the prophecies inculcated many years earlier by the Bene Gesserit Missionaria Protectiva. Such elements as Jessica's response to Shadout Mapes when shown the crysknife (though partially accidental), Paul's ability to fit the stillsuit to himself perfectly on first wearing, and his choice of words in response to a number of situations begin the process of fitting Paul into the messiah-pattern established by the Missionaria Protectiva. These provide the basis on which Paul and Jessica are taken in by the Fremen society initially, and they also foreshadow Paul's eventual rise to power among them; were it not for the fact that Paul fits into this pattern, and impresses Kynes in the process, that initial foothold which is so necessary would apparently have been denied.

The Harkonnen invasion, the death of Leto, and the defeat of the Atreides forces combine to cast Paul completely out of the kind of life that he has previously known and provides the goal of his quest: revenge for the treachery, and the standing-by which allowed it, for the death of his father. Equally important to his development, however, is the scene in the stilltent just after Paul and Jessica have escaped the guards who were to kill them. In the first place, the stilltent functions as a symbol of the womb: it is a totally enclosed space designed to retain the life-giving water; its opening is a sphincter which dilates to let them out (and in); in the tent,

Paul is in extremely close contact with his mother. However, it is not such elements as these which are most significant in making his emergence from the tent a rebirth; rather, it is what happens within Paul that is significant, for he emerges as a far different person than when he went in. As he sits in the tent, his knees hugged tightly (close to the fetal position), he reviews his past and arranges the data that he has gained. As he points out, this is the working of his Mentat powers, but it is also something added to them; that is, while it is his Mentat power which allows/forces the computation of his data, it seems to be his Bene Gesserit training in the observation of the tiniest clues which provides much of the data on which his computations are based. Either of these steps would be a significant development for Paul; however, he has already shown an ability to focus and use his Bene Gesserit awareness, although not with such complete recall, so that the new functioning of his Mentat abilities is the more significant. Yet more important, of course, is his ability to link these two disciplines, on the one hand giving him more complete data than available to most Mentats and on the other hand giving far greater ability to handle and interpret his data than any Bene Gesserit. In this state, he sees things more clearly and quickly than his mother does, one more indication of his developing powers; on the other hand, the element of self-pity that he shows suggests that he must still develop in other directions. Nevertheless, during this stage he reaches a more accurate portrait of their situation and about the planet than he had before or than his mother is able to construct.

Paul's development in the "womb" does not stop at this point, for in the midst of his computations, his prescient awareness is brought into focus for the first time in a waking condition, throwing open the many possible avenues of the future and adding more data for his computations. The integration of these three threads is important, but is less significant than the fact that it frightens Paul enough to force himself to consider what he actually is. He moves from sheer terror at feeling himself a freak or a monster to anger at his mother for bearing him and training him so that exposure to the spice could bring the change in him to consciousness. He moves on to recognize what Arrakis will become, that his mother is tremendously vulnerable, and that Baron Harkonnen is his grandfather. He rejects the notion that he is the kwisatz haderach toward which the Bene Gesserit have been working, instead being something quite unexpected. As he realizes that he is a seed (a concept which becomes quite important in viewing *Dune Messiah*), he also realizes the purpose which he must fulfill, sowing that seed into the fertile ground around him. He recognizes the Jihad to come, though he does not like the idea at all. Finally, he foresees that to the Fremen, he will be called Muad'dib, The One Who Points The Way. Whereas he had previously been unable to mourn his father, regret for which makes a refrain throughout this scene, with this last realization he is finally able to weep. Since he could not weep earlier because of the computerlike working of his mind, the fact that he now can seems to signal the integration of these new abilities and this new knowledge into his total personality—at least far enough for him to function as a human being. Thus, he is ready to emerge from the stilltent and to emerge from boyhood as a leader; when they do emerge, his mother automatically falls into her son's orbit.

Almost immediately following his rebirth in the stilltent, which consolidates his abilities and focuses them so he will be able to bring them to bear on the business of survival, Paul must face the first of three tests. To pass this test, and to survive, Paul must pilot an ornithopter skillfully enough to escape Harkonnen pursuit and to fly through one of the savage sandstorms for which Arrakis is noted, using the sandstorm to shake off pursuit. In order to get through the sandstorm successfully, Paul must use his Bene Gesserit powers of observation and his Mentat powers of calculation in tandem to discover the path through the storm; however, this is not enough, for he must also use the speed and coordination gained through his weapons training to act immediately and precisely on the computations derived from his other abilities. Although the ornithopter is damaged in the storm, the fact that both he and Jessica emerge from it unhurt is sufficient to indicate that Paul has successfully met his first test during the quest proper. This test also introduces two lines of development that mark the direction and terms of his quest: the growth of his political influence, and the growth of his ability to live the Fremen life and to become one with the desert. Thus, before he and Jessica can even get the ornithopter, Paul must convince Kynes that he is worthy of protection; it takes him so little time to bring himself to ducal stature in the eyes of Kynes that Jessica remarks on the ease with which the Atreides manage to do such things so thoroughly. Not only does Paul win them the chance to escape in the ornithopter but he also gains a message from Kynes to the Fremen asking safe conduct for them, without which Paul's success in riding the storm would go for naught.

The other line of development is more central to the novel as a whole. If he and Jessica are to survive to complete the quest, they must learn the Fremen ways. By the time that they meet the Fremen, led by Stilgar, Paul has already moved several steps in this direction. He has obviously learned a great deal about the nature of the sandstorms as he flew through one; not only does he survive the experience, but he also confidently uses just such a storm as a weapon later when they attack the Emperor's forces. In addition, as they cross the sand when they leave the ornithopter to the sandworms, Paul learns how they must walk if they are to avoid death in the jaws of the worms; he learns that the terrain enforces its own rhythms and humans must abide by those rhythms if they are to live. Finally, he learns that great care must be taken in the desert and that the slightest slip might be fatal when Jessica is caught in the sandslide and some of their supplies lost. This sandslide, incidentally, is significant in two other ways, for it brings Jessica to the point of firmly telling Paul that he needs to continue his lessons in the Bene Gesserit disciplines (such further development along these lines is implied but not directly shown through the rest of the novel) and it brings Paul to the point where he can admit that he has been an active party to whatever has been done to him, an admission which suggests that he now is ready to follow up on that training in a conscious fashion. Success in all these things is not an end in itself; it would seem more accurate to view these events as qualifying Paul for the next test which he must overcome if he is to complete his quest.

The second test centers around Paul's fight with Jamis, although a number of other elements cluster around this fight. The fight comes about because Jamis, apparently the only one out of the tribe, is reluctant to accept the word of Kynes and to accept the barely supported possibility that Paul is the Lisan al-Gaib (Jessica's fighting ability and the fact that she is a Bene Gesserit both fit into the prophecy, and she is able to pick up details of the ritual just after they are brought into the sietch). Although Jamis claims that his motivation is to test their role in the prophecy, his hot temper and the fact that Paul managed to knock him down and get by him seem to be equally important to him. To win this fight, Paul must do two things that he has never done before, fight without a shield and kill a man. Because of his shield training, his offense is too slow; he is also reluctant to kill a man until he learns that he must, according to Fremen law. Under the circumstances, he finds that the only way to accomplish this is to turn Jamis's body against himself. When he has successfully passed this test, both he and Jessica are officially brought into the troop, which paves the way for further learning about the Fremen way and about life on the desert, both of which culminate in the third test, riding the Maker.

Approximately three years pass between Paul's second and third tests. In that interval, a number of things happen that solidify his position among the Fremen, both as a member of their troop and as the Lisan al-Gaib, that bring further awareness of his special powers, and that prepare for his assumption of his ducal recognition and the subsequent annexation of the Imperial throne. One of the first things that happens immediately after the fight is that Jessica challenges his pride for successfully killing Jamis; while this does not deter him from killing again, it does cause him to be aware of the destructive possibilities and to weigh them against other factors. Perhaps the best example of this comes in *Dune Messiah*, when Paul reveals full awareness of the destruction wrought by the Jihad and the numbers of lives that have been lost. Also shortly after the fight and even more shortly after he has been brought officially into the troop, Paul enhances his position among them by giving water to the dead during the funeral ceremony for Jamis. Although the process is not detailed in the novel, it is on this base that Paul begins to build his influence among the Fremen. Even before he has passed this third test, which formally initiates him into full Fremen manhood, Paul has become a leader among them, leading them into battle against the Harkonnen and being listened to with respect in council. One of the factors in his apparently steady movement toward power involves the prophecy of the Lisan al-Gaib. The Fremen, of course, seem to be more than ready to accept him as such, for even such a small thing as choosing a name sets off comments about the Lisan al-Gaib, while his tears at Jamis's funeral, though they are involuntary, nevertheless are sacred within the Fremen religion and produce awe among them. As mentioned, the fact that Jessica is a Bene Gesserit helps situate them into the prophecy; when she (and Alia) becomes a Reverend Mother, that situation is greatly enhanced. In addition, Paul seems to become caught up in his own myth a number of times, when he feels his terrible purpose building up within himself and when he sees himself as a pivot point in the course of the Empire; at one point, he feels that he has missed an essential decision and that he has, therefore, committed himself to becoming the Lisan al-Gaib and all that that implies. During this time, Paul also seems to learn more about the nature and the limits of his prescient powers. Even as early as the walk across the desert with Jessica, he noted that his vision of this event included Duncan Idaho, which was not true of the reality. Before his battle with Jamis, he experiences the complications possible within his vision of time and realizes that the expenditure of energy needed for his prescient visions also changes what he sees, introducing an indeterminacy into the vision. In addition to this, he sees the variables that affect the outcome and the many possible futures that can result. Perhaps the most important element of his prescient visions is the fact that he keeps seeing the jihad, and bends many of his efforts toward finding ways to avoid it if he can; the fact that he cannot resolve this and that the vision becomes muddy when he tries to probe into the jihad and beyond seem to be a major motivating force in his later drinking of the Water of Life. Nevertheless, within the limits of his powers at this time, Paul does learn a great deal about the nature of his gift, its limitations and its uses.

In a way, the third test that Paul undergoes seems to be to one side of the main line of his development, for it is a peculiarly Fremen ritual, even more so than the fight with Jamis. This appearance, however, is deceiving. The entire process is a ritual initiation into manhood, particularly appropriate to Arrakis, for if he (or any other young man of the Fremen) can master a Maker, call one and ride it, he has the freedom of the desert. One might also point toward the phallic nature of the worm and suggest that mastery in that regard is also very appropriate to an initiation into manhood. It is also interesting to note that Paul is given hooks that have never failed by one of the troop, a feature similar to gifts and other aids provided in many heroic romances. However, this test has other implications, of which Paul is fully aware. Not only does successfully passing it give him the full rights and responsibilities of a Fremen male, but it also strengthens his rule over them. Beyond this, however, he sees a parallel between mastering the Maker and mastering his inward sight; thus, riding the Maker provides a direct line into his death and rebirth through the Water of Life/Death. There are several things of interest about the test itself. In the first place, Paul has never seen or heard of a Maker as large as the one that he calls. Second, as Jessica did after the fight with Jamis, Stilger indicates the mistakes Paul made in mounting the worm in order to dampen the flush of success and to urge care in the future that will insure survival. Third, Paul formally announces that this day marks a change in his life, that before this he had been a child who had a cork sealing off his world that has now been removed, expanding his possibilities of action. Finally, at the end of this ride, the fact that Paul must come to grips with the troop's expectation that he will call Stilgar out for leadership is brought in the open between them. In a sense, the meeting at which he turns aside the necessity of challenging Stilgar to the death is the second half of this test, for it would seem that many of the troop have been waiting only for Paul to pass into manhood before forcing the issue. To do this, he uses several methods which show his development. First, he accepts the religious mantle deliberately, the title of the Lisan al-Gaib. Then he uses the intonations of the Voice, one indication that his training in the Bene Gesserit way has continued since the sandslide when they entered the desert. Finally, he puts on his father's ducal ring and claims the whole of Arrakis as his rightful fief. All the while, he has been challenging them on their own grounds, forcing them to rethink what they are demanding that he do. In all these ways, but especially by raising himself above the level of the individual troop and sietch, he makes himself free to retain the strength and wisdom of a valuable ally while still keeping the troop happy and following him. In addition, he again, perhaps unconsciously, follows the prophecy and further strengthens his position. Not only does Paul successfully pass the third test, but he also turns liabilities into assets as he does so.

When he passes this third test, it is as though he has finally become ready to transcend the state to which these tests have brought him, to lay claim to his full abilities and powers. All that separates the third test from a second experience of death and rebirth is a short period during which he reconciles his mother and Gurney Halleck. Although he seems to have thought about the Maker and tasting the Water of Life before, his definite decision to do so comes only after his reconciliation has been effected. It comes some three years after his emergence from the stilltent, and, where his experience in the stilltent involved another person, the experience of the Water of Life is undertaken alone. In part, he does this because he feels a need to clarify his prescient vision and to increase his control over it. He is also aware, of course, that if he survives this test, it will mark him as the Kwisatz Haderach and confirm him in the role of the Lisan al-Gaib. It is interesting to note that this death and rebirth is described externally — we see only his decision to do so and his waking, with a subsequent suggestion of what he has experienced — rather than internally, as was the scene in the stilltent. After he has taken the Water of Life, which can also be the Water of Death, Paul lies as though dead for three weeks (the period of time is clearly related to the three days Christ spent in the tomb, as well as to the three-fold repetitions frequently found in heroic adventures on all levels), hanging on to life only by the slenderest thread. After he has been awakened, his first indication of what he has experienced is his suggestion that he has been many places and seen many things. Since we have already been given an impression of Jessica's experience in transmitting the poison, her terror when Paul forces her into rapport with him is also suggestive of the great differences between her experience and his, as well as of the violence and chaos of what he has experienced. Once he has done this, he explains that what he has faced is both of the ancient forces within Man, the force that gives and the force that takes; it has been previously established in the novel that the Bene Gesserit can only experience the force that gives, unable to penetrate into experience of the force that takes and still live. In addition to experiencing both forces and to gaining the ability to be many places at once, Paul realizes that he is at the fulcrum, unable to give without taking, unable to take without giving. For the second time in the novel, Paul sees himself as a pivot point, a figure who can change the direction of things. This, of course, has a direct bearing on the coming battle; Paul's experience has not been only with the forces of his mind, but also with what he calls the Now, all time existing in the present moment, for he is completely aware of the fact that the Emperor himself is waiting above the planet (he has, remember, just come out of his trance and has had no time to receive intelligence reports), as well as who is with the Emperor. This scene of rebirth ends with Paul giving the orders that will make it possible to totally destroy the spice, using the Water of Life as the Water of Death to set off a chain reaction to kill the Makers and hence eliminate the spice; through his experience of the Water of Life, he has come to grips with the nature of Life and Death, and he is ready to use this knowledge to complete his quest and to plant the seed that he is in the soil around him, thus changing the direction of human history. It should also be noted that one of the Fremen, Otheym, has been listening while Paul gives his explanation of what he has undergone; when he reports to the other Fremen that Paul has taken the Water of Life and survived and that he has seen many things that other men may not, Paul's role as the Lisan al-Gaib will be firmly cemented so that the hero and the messiah will be identical in the action that follows in both *Dune* and *Dune Messiah*.

In the process of transmuting the Water of Life from a deadly poison to a substance which opens to him forces of mind previously inaccessible and allows him to bridge time and space, Paul Atreides is transfigured. That is, he gains the full powers to which he was bred and trained, and, in so doing, he rises a step beyond normal human kind; he has truly become the Lisan al-Gaib. Furthermore, it is the final step which readies him to complete his quest and claim his reward, to meet the forces of the Empire with some assurance that he will defeat them. There is little doubt of the outcome, but the defeat must be formally accomplished to clearly mark the victory of the hero over the forces of villainy and to establish Paul's claim in the eyes of those over whom he will rule. Once the initial battle is fought and the forces of the Emperor are effectively paralyzed, the stage is set for Paul's recognition as the Atreides heir and as the successor to the Imperial throne. Paul's possession of the ducal signet is one sign of his identity, but even more important is the fact that Shaddam IV addresses him as a kinsman when they first meet; this allows him to press his claim openly and to legitimately act as he does against the Emperor. It also opens the way for Irulan, the Bene Gesserit daughter trained to be the wife of Shaddam's successor, to argue Paul's case. Between the initial proposal that Paul marry Irulan and succeed Shaddam on the Imperial throne and the final disposition of the question, another matter must be taken care of: the false hero must be punished and any potential opposition eliminated. Feyd-Rautha Harkonnen represents the other side of the line through which the Bene Gesserit hoped to achieve the kwisatz haderach; had Paul been the girl Jessica was ordered to produce, the son of that daughter and Feyd-Rautha was to have been the Kwisatz Haderach. In addition, Feyd-Rautha had been trained by his grandfather, the old Baron Harkonnen, toward the end of succeeding to the throne. Thus, it is necessary for Paul to fight yet one more battle to establish his claim firmly and incontestably. It is significant that the battle which he could not have won is never fought, for Count Fenring recognizes Paul for what he is and realizes that Paul has recognized what he might have been. This entire confrontation with the Emperor and his forces is also necessary on several other counts. First, it provides the basis on which the Space Guild is forced to recognize Paul's ability to destroy the spice and thus destroy them; this gives him control over them and minimizes any opposition they might have mounted against him. Second, it convinces the Reverend Mother Gaius Helen Mohiam that Paul is indeed the kwisatz haderach, and perhaps something more, and that she did indeed make a mistake when she passed lightly over this possibility; furthermore, it makes quite clear that the Bene Gesserit will never be able to control him and use him for their own purposes. Finally, this confrontation dramatizes the punishment of the villain, of the Emperor who used guile and subterfuge to eliminate Duke Leto, perhaps the only man in the Empire who could have threatened the Emperor's power, though there is no indication that he wished to do so. His throne is stripped from him, his entire CHOAM Company holdings are to be taken from him, and he is banished to Salusa Secundus, the prison planet. In addition, Princess Irulan is to become Paul's wife, though, ironically, never his mate.

Thus, *Dune* chronicles the course of Paul Atreides through the first two phases of Heroic Romance, from his advent into this universe and his initiation into his heroic condition through his series of trials which help him to develop his heroic abilities to his final recognition and reward. The final scenes of the novel, of course, demonstrate that his training has been successful, that his trials have been overcome and the knowledge gained from them put to effective use, and that he is a hero not only fit to reign over the Empire but also to change its course.

If *Dune* chronicles these phases of the Heroic Romance, then *Dune Messiah* chronicles the last phase of the hero's career, the phase in which he consolidates his position and awaits the final, culminating events of his life, which often includes both passing on his position to a worthy successor and being united with the divine. In addition, this phase of Heroic Romance deals with the last, convulsive opposition of the hero's enemies; it shows his ways of dealing with the opposition, with his actions frequently solitary and full of guile; and it concludes with his death, which is a transcendence of this world. Because of the nature of these events, this phase is often quieter and more ceremonial than the first two phases. Though this description fits many, many stories, both traditional and modern, it could easily have been developed simply from reading *Dune Messiah*.

Quite obviously, both the last phase of traditional Romances, when it is included as a part of the story, and *Dune Messiah* build upon the gains the hero has already made, although they do not always begin at the point at which the second phase left off (that is, at the point at which the hero gains his reward), instead focusing on his last, significant acts. Of course, the intervening actions are normally summarized for the reader. Thus, the action in *Dune Messiah* begins some twelve years after Paul's confrontation with Shaddam IV. In those twelve years, the jihad predicted in *Dune* has taken place, with Fremen forces sweeping from planet to planet; indeed, during the period covered by this novel, the jihad still continues, though the impulse behind it is dying rapidly. It has, however, served several purposes: 1) most important, it has helped Paul to create and to establish his empire, for no planet has been able to stand against the Fremen; 2) it has spread the religion of Muad'dib throughout the system, both through its Fremen worshippers and through the more formal action of the Qizarate missionaries; 3) it has opened the way to change, destroying the old patterns and forcing new ones; and 4) it has thoroughly mixed the gene pool, far more thoroughly than the patient work of the Bene Gesserit could ever hope for. These last two purposes seem to look beyond Paul Atreides, for they prepare the ground in which the seed that is Paul is planted; the fruition of that planting will necessarily come after his death. The first two, however, are directly connected with Paul's consolidation of his position, for although he seized power from the Emperor at the end of *Dune*, it is necessary to enforce that seizure and to bring the lesser figures solidly under his reign; not only is this done physically and politically through the Fremen invasions, it is also done religiously through the Qizarate.

The portion of the human universe which remained untouched by this dual thrust was small. Thus, with few exceptions—the Tupile Treaty and the submission of the Ixian Confederacy are the most prominent—the matters to which Paul gives his attention are not matters of consolidation but matters of conspiracy against himself, his Empire, and his heirs. The major groups involved in this conspiracy are, of course, those whose power and influence have been severely affected by Paul's rise to power: the Bene Gesserit, represented by the Reverend Mother Gaius Helen Mohiam, who also has personal motives for being involved; the Space Guild, represented by Edric; the ex-Emperor, represented by Irulan, who is also, of course, a Bene Gesserit and who also has personal motives for desiring the success of the conspiracy. The Bene Tleilaxu, represented by Scytale the Face Dancer, are also a part of this conspiracy, though their grievance against Paul is unclear; in many ways, intellectual curiosity—about the reactions of a kwisatz haderach, about the revival of a ghola's memories, and about the interplay of political forces—seems to be their primary motivation for involvement. In addition to these major forces, at least three of which have a long-standing quarrel with Paul, the leaders of the Qizarate hierarchy have also joined the forces against him, for he has stifled their drive toward independent power and the ways in which they can build their religion around him. Fremen themselves, the Qizarate hierarchy bring into the conspiracy many of the disaffected Fremen, those who look back on the old ways with nostalgia, those who find the changes too rapid to assimilate. The largest share of *Dune Messiah,* then, is devoted to exploring the various aspects and moves of this conspiracy and the ways in which Paul Muad'dib, the Mentat Emperor, deals with them.

Two things about the conspiracy are quite clear; in terms of the total population and of the total space governed by Paul, the conspiracy is very small, very limited, although some of the groups represent a good deal of power; furthermore, in order to achieve their ends, they must necessarily come to Paul, and cluster around him, for he personally is their target. In view of these facts, it is hardly surprising that Paul is aware of the conspiracy, as well as many of the moves that conspirators make, almost from the beginning. What may seem surprising is the way that Paul handles this knowledge. That is, he seems to make a game of cat and mouse of it, making his moves and waiting patiently for theirs; the final outcome is not in doubt in its essence, though the details may be clouded. However, Paul's actions in handling this conspiracy are very much in accord with the actions of the hero in the third phase of Romance. Both Paul and the "typical" hero await the culminating events of their careers. Given his prescient powers, Paul is aware of what those culminating events are likely to be; more precisely, he is aware of which set of culminating events, out of the many possibilities he "sees," are the most favorable to allowing his seed to be nurtured and grow. Thus, much of his action, and even his lack of action, is directed at bringing the various forces involved into the alignment which will produce a particular set of culminating events. One of the factors involved, of course, is the birth of his child; clearly, he does not have total control of the situation, nor total sight of the culmination of his career, for Chani gives birth to twins, and knows she will do so quite early in the novel. Nevertheless, the birth of this child (these children) is necessary for the fruition, so that a major cause of Paul's delay in dealing directly with the major forces in the conspiracy is the need to gain time in order that Chani's pregnancy can come to term. In addition, the time gained allows other, apparently necessary, events to take place. The first of these is the delivery of the ghola Hayt; the second is Paul's being blinded after the visit to Otheym, in which the dwarf Bijaz is gained; the third is beginning down those within and around the Qizarate who conspire against Paul and his house. It is also noteworthy that in these dealings and these actions Paul, like the hero of third-phase Romance, most often acts on his own, without consulting others and without revealing his knowledge or his purposes to them; this is carried to the point that he does not even confide in Chani, because of his drive to bring events to the envisaged clumination without interference, however well-meaning.

In the typical pattern of third-phase Heroic Romance, the hero also descends into hell, during which he becomes more aware of other powers in the universe, gains some kind of knowledge (often of the future), and is prepared for his assumption of his divine role; this descent need not be actual, but rather it can be implied through the hero's withdrawal or it can be symbolic. It can be argued that this feature appears in *Dune*, when Paul transmutes the Water of Life, for not only does he penetrate the chaotic force (very like hell), he also gains greater knowledge of the future and very shortly afterward accepts the religious mantle among the Fremen.

Nevertheless, in an oblique and symbolic way, Paul's visit to Otheym's house and its aftermath also serve some of the functions served by the more traditional descent into hell. Otheym's house is in the worst part of the city, the overcrowded slums; to reach it, Paul must journey downward from the palace, both physically and "socially." It is the stone burner, however, which provides the symbolic touch of hell, with its flames and radiation, with its violation of the Great Convention, and with the chaotic conditions it creates. From this encounter, Paul gains several things in the form of the dwarf Bijaz, in whose mind are recorded the names of all the traitors and their acts. Also in the form of Bijaz, Paul is given the key that will unlock the Duncan Idaho memories in the ghola Hayt; there are strong indications that Idaho, along with Alia, is important to the continuity of events following Paul's death. In addition, Paul's vision of the future is solidified by this event; even though he is physically blinded by the radiation of the stone burner, he is able to act as though sighted, to name the people around him and describe their clothing, from that point until Chani's death. This ability to "see," though sightless, adds to the legend surrounding Paul and adds to the awe that is accorded him. Finally, this scene and the other consequences prepare for Paul's apotheosis; though his stature in life is godlike, when he walks into the desert to fulfill the Fremen law, he cements the Fremen belief in him and creates the conditions for his final deification.

Thus, the final hours of Paul's life are far more eventful than the rest of the novel. The birth of the twins, one male and one female, signals the beginning of the culmination of his career, for now he is sure that the seed which he is can grow and develop. In addition, he now has someone of equal stature with himself—greater, really—to whom he can pass leadership, confident that what he has begun will be continued. With the birth of his children and the succession assured, Paul is able to face the situation in which Hayt will either kill him or regain his identity as Duncan Idaho. With Idaho's support, Paul is able to face Scytale of the Tleilaxu and to refuse the temptations he offers, as well as refusing to surrender to his threats. Using the freely offered eyes of his newborn son—already aware and possessed of more powers than Paul—he is able to end the threat posed by Scytale and by the conspiracy; Scytale's death breaks the conspiracy, leaving the others to be dealt with later. Finally, when Bijaz tries to tempt him, Paul has him killed. With this act, Paul is freed of the terrible purpose he felt gripping him throughout *Dune,* and he is freed of the compulsive power of his prescient vision. He is free to end his life, to follow the Fremen law and walk into the desert—and into myth—to become one with Shai-hulud.

Under any circumstances, it is quite clear that the action in *Dune Messiah* is a completion of the action begun in *Dune.* When the two novels are compared against the pattern of Heroic Romance, however, the unity and continuity between them becomes even clearer, for the third phase of Romance — the phase described by *Dune Messiah* — is the logical culmination of the first two phases if the vision of the career of the hero is pressed past his initial triumph. Nevertheless, Herbert himself views *Dune Messiah* as a pivotal novel; the successor to a hero, after all, is a subject worthy of attention in his (their) own right(s). For *that* culmination, however, we must wait until Herbert completes the third novel in the sequence.

THE GODMAKERS
1972

The Godmakers is a more single-minded exploration of the messianic impulse that made up a part of the total exploration in *Dune*. Although some of the complexity and richness of the earlier novel is lost, there are gains in clarity of focus and in detail within this area. Thus, Lewis Orne starts out in this novel as a fairly ordinary young man, even though he seems to be above average in a number of ways. Apparently randomly selected, the process of Religious Engineering on Amel, as part of the training of candidates for religious knowledge, makes him a psi focus. This, in turn, necessitates that he go through a series of tests which both determine his fitness to be a god and teach him the powers and resources at his command and control. Because these elements are focused clearly and in greater detail, this novel can profitably be read in conjunction with *Dune* and *Dune Messiah,* for it may shed some light on what happens to Paul Atreides in the course of those novels. In the course of this, quite naturally, there is some exploration of what qualities a god might have, what powers, and what he might do with them. In addition to these explorations, there is some exploration of the background society which provides the basis for Orne's progress and the action sequences which provide the continuity between the experiences that make him a god. Primarily, Herbert explores the wisdom of using violence to insure, to enforce, peace and of possible alternatives to this. All of these elements are well integrated; *The Godmakers* is a solid, interesting novel, not far below the class containing *Dune* and a very few other science-fiction novels.

As in *Dune,* but in a much more direct way, the element in *The Godmakers* that provides the framework and the impetus for the other elements is the development of the central character. None of the thematic elements can finally be separated from that development, since they are focused primarily through Lewis Orne's consciousness, but it is nevertheless possible to trace that development in its main outlines before other factors are brought to bear, though some background is necessary first. The most important aspect of this background is the class in Religious Engineering on Amel, more popularly known as godmaking. What the demonstration pictured early in the novel does is to focus psi-energies on some object (it need not be human), to bring the god out of chaos each time this is done. However, they only know how to set these forces in motion; they do not know what object the psi-energies will focus on and they do not have any control over what they have created. However, through the visions that accompany this process they, and the reader, have some sense of things that will be involved in bringing the god to reality. This vision includes Ag Emolirdo, the Abbod's brother and Lewis Orne's first instructor in how to use his psi powers, one finger pressing a button on a green box, an act which is described in the very first section of the book, and the words of the Shriggar, the death lizard of Lewis Orne's homeworld of Chargon. Thus, by the time the reader sees the three visions with the Abbod, he already has two of the clues necessary to connect Lewis Orne with this process of godmaking. In addition, the Shriggar names the perils to be faced and outlines the process through which Lewis Orne must go. That is, he mentions the game of war, which makes up the first large section of the novel, as Orne discovers the violent intentions under apparent peacefulness on Hamal, the city of glass, which constitutes the second major section of the book, as Orne makes contact with the natives Gienah, the time for politics, which involves the third major section of the novel, while Orne is a guest at the home of High Commissioner Bullone, and, finally, the time for the priests to fear what they have created, which is the focus of Orne's testing in the fourth major section of the novel. The Shriggar also points out that all of these steps must be gone through before the process of making a god is complete and that there is no guarantee that their potential god will survive these tests. The final important aspect of this background is the quotation from *The Amel Handbook,* quoted before the first part of the story, which suggests what it is that the potential god must learn through the tests he must face. Through the game of war he must become aware of hidden aggression; through his meeting with the natives of Gienah, he must come to an understanding of purpose in the animal form; before he can engage in politics, he must undergo the experience of death and be reborn; and the process of rebirth will come to culmination in the ordeal he must face on Amel, which will also give the priests cause to fear what they have created. These elements give a sense of unity and direction to the novel by suggesting some of the relationships between the parts. They also outline the development of Lewis Orne and provide the framework for interpreting that development and its stages.

The early life of Lewis Orne is not particularly important to this novel, for in a sense his development does not begin until he signals the I-A from Hamal. There are two reasons for saying this: first, it is this amount which is one facet of the vision during the godmaking, and second, it is this moment which precipitates him from his repetitive dream into a waking series of events which remind him of his dreams. Even so, some of the early events in his life are given, and these events do lead toward the path forecast by the Shriggar. He was born on Chargon, under the star Gemma, into the family of the Chargonian Member to the governing body of the Galactic League. His entire family was politically oriented, and his mother was a major factor in grooming him to take over when it was learned that his father would die soon. Because he did not like the compromises necessitated by politics, to be directed by women, and the urgings of his recurrent dream, Lewis Orne left home when he was seventeen to enlist in the Federation Marines; when he was nineteen years old, he transferred into the Rediscovery and Re-education Service. After five years of training, he was sent to Hamal on his first solo assignment. Ten weeks later, he pushed the button, the act which was seen in the vision, which brought the course of his life from dreams into waking reality, and which started his real education by bringing him into contact with the I-A Service (Investigation-Adjustment).

When Lewis Orne pushes the panic button on his signal set, he brings the I-A onto Hamal because he *feels* undercurrents on the planet are at odds with the professions of the people and the surfaces of their actions, but he is unable to verbalize exactly what it is that makes him feel this way or how the various things that he can point to are indications that the Hamalites are a basically violent and warlike people. Thus, although he has a feeling that there is something on this planet that needs to be more completely investigated, he cannot be said to be aware of secret aggression. His questioning by Umbo Stetson and the tour they take of the countryside provide the education he needs to bring these feelings to meaningful awareness; that is, Stetson points to a number of facts about the planet, many of which Orne had felt were at odds with the professions of peacefulness made by the people, and explicitly shows him how to interpret them. For example, Stetson points out that military roads most often are built on high ground, while farm roads usually follow the lower ground, or that spyglasses are usually developed in connection with long range weapons. Many of the other aspects of the society are similarly explained. By the time that their tour of the countryside is over and the I-A call is made, Orne has become aware of secret aggression and is ready to move on to the next step in his development. In part, this readiness is shown by the fact that Stetson drafts him into the I-A, which is also necessary so that he can come into contact with the dwellers in the city of glass, as forecast by the Shriggar. A more important indicator of his readiness for the next step can be seen in the sureness with which he handles himself in that rather tight situation.

The next of the series of events prophesied by the Shriggar, the contact with the dwellers in the glass city which is to give Lewis Orne understanding of purpose in the animal form, begins immediately following the conclusion of the first episode, with no transitional material at all. Although this is a legitimate technique in fiction, it does suggest the magazine origin of the stories involved. The natives of Gienah pose an entirely different problem than did the natives of Hamal: they are an alien race, although their evolution seems in many ways parallel to ours. It is not the fact that they are alien that poses the problem, however, but rather the fact that they have captured a space ship belonging to R&R and then forged a request for an agent-instructor. The problem is given to Orne, who was sufficiently with R&R to be on the master lists on the *Delphinus;* he must determine whether or not these aliens can be cleared for human conduct, with the alternative being completely destroying the planet. As if this were not difficult enough, the entire task must be completed within five days, the longest period of time that the information can be kept from the politicians. He does, however, manage to discover what motivates the Gienahans, what keys he can use to bring them into peaceful contact with humans, and where they have hidden the captured ship. There is little action in this section of the novel, other than the moment that the native leader drops on the hood of Orne's vehicle and the moment when Orne lifts off the ground with a force of several gravities, using his heavy gravity planet strength to disarm the native leader and gain his respect; mostly, the leader and Orne talk as the vehicle moves from the point of interception to near the city of glass, but through this conversation and his analysis of what he knows of the language and the people, Orne is able to make his discoveries.

In his explanation to Stetson after he has been returned to the ship, he makes it clear that he has gained the insight required by this second test. That is, beginning with the fact that the word the natives used for themselves was different from what would normally have been expected, Orne postulated a super-structure guiding their concepts that was directly related to their animal shape. He also applies what he knows of history (human), what he has seen of their actions, and what he has heard of their language. From this he determined that they were newly emerged from the primitive, that they are extremely dependent on their city for species continuation, that they were night hunters accustomed to dropping on their prey from above, and that, therefore, the *Delphinus* had to be hidden on a mountain on the dark side of their moon. Although he does not care for either of the alternatives facing him, his sensibilities and his compassion for the aliens (or anyone about to come under the Occupation Force of the I-A), he finds this preferable to exterminating them, as Stetson would have liked to do. That he comes out of this adventure alive is, of course, the primary indication that Orne has passed his second test on the way to godhood, but his being accepted as a senior field agent also, and more formally, marks the achievement.

The next stage of the testing that Lewis Orne must undergo on his way to achieving godhood has two phases. The first phase is his virtual death during the Sheleb Incident; that is, he is as close to actual physical death as a being could be without actually being dead, totally supported by the mechanisms of the crechepod and not expected to live even with that support. This, then, is his experience with death which is spoken of in *The Amel Handbook;* in nearly all heroic advantures, however, death is primarily a preparation for rebirth. In the specific case of Lewis Orne, both the death and the rebirth take place on two levels. On the physical level, he is virtually dead, but somehow manages to use the resources of the crechepod to recover enough so that surgical techniques can be used to bring him to the point where he can regrow, with medical help, the parts of himself which were destroyed. More important is the fact that his physical virtual death also parallels the death or re-examination of some of his ideas about himself and the role that he has been playing. As he recovers physically, his thinking also takes a new direction. Specifically, he begins to wonder about the nature of war and of the kind of repression of war and violent impulses undertaken by the I-A; he feels choked by things that he once accepted—and he comes to a new definition of existence. Thus, the rebirth of his mind parallels the rebirth of his flesh.

In a sense, the fruits of this rebirth do not really show themselves until very near the end of the second phase of this third stage of his testing and preparation for godhood. The second phase is the time for politics predicted by the Shriggar. After he is invited to recuperate in the home of High Commissioner Bullone, the I-A asks him to do some investigating and to analyze the situation there, for they have gotten wind of a political conspiracy centering in, they think, the High Commissioner's daughter Diana. Although he would rather not, he agrees to do so. In the process, however, several things happen, perhaps the least of which is his falling in love with Diana. He does discover that a conspiracy exists, he determines its nature and how it works, and he finds a way to resolve the problem created without any use of violence or the threat of violence. Most important, however, he discovers a number of things about himself. He discovers that he is a Nathian and that his sex was determined so that he would be able to continue his father's career of public service, even though a number of years would pass. The fact that his mother determined his sex at conception both links Lewis Orne with Paul Atreides and provides the unusual birth so common to heroes and gods. The other major thing that he learns about himself is that simply by wishing it, he can transfer the transceiver implanted in his neck to the deepest ocean on the planet; in short, he has psi power. All of these things, but especially his discovery of his psi abilities, pave the way into the next stage of Lewis Orne's progress toward becoming a god.

This last stage also has two phases, the seven tests which he must pass and his realization of what he is. In order to do these things, he must go to the planet Amel, the ecumenical center of all religions in the known universe and also the center for all but the most preliminary psi training; but before he can go, he also needs that preliminary training and he must be summoned to Amel, for no one goes there uninvited. Once again, he is asked to make his visit a dual purpose visit, for all the priests on Amel are opposed to the Investigation-Adjustment Service, and the I-A wants to know why. When he arrives on Amel, he is told that he must be tested in seven ways, and he must pass these tests before he will be able to see the Abbod, who is his goal for both of his purposes on Amel. He must undergo the test of faith, the test of the two faces of miracle, the test of dogma and ceremony, the test of religious ideal, the tests of his ethics, service of life, and personal mystique. It is pointed out to him that there is no necessary order to these tests and that they are not necessarily separated. However, for each of these tests he must face some aspect of himself which he has not faced before or learn something about mankind which he has not known.

In the first test he undergoes, the test of faith, he must discover what he has faith in, and the sort of faith that will banish fear; in the process he must also face his own fears and those of others. Finally, he discovers that he is capable of casting the soul of another into hell, but he also realizes that the ability to do a thing does not confer the right to do it, thus learning to censor his will. When he does all of these things, he has passed the first of his tests. The second test he undergoes is that of the two faces of miracle. The first thing that he discovers about himself during this test is a deep and abiding hate that has long been suppressed in his conscious mind. He also learns that the universe is a single whole and that good and evil are two sides of a coin, dependent on perspective and motivation for definition; that is, one person cannot determine whether or not another is good or evil. Although the fact that he is alive after any one of these tests is sufficient evidence that he has passed it, his guide affirms that Lewis Orne now understands the two faces of miracle, but also that through this ordeal he has shown a personal mystique and an ethic in service to life. Consequently, by the time his second ordeal has been completed, he has passed five of the tests. Immediately, with no chance for rest, he passes on to the next (third) ordeal, that of dogma and ceremony. During this ordeal he discovers the psi field arising, not from machines as had been the case in the previous two ordeals, but from the mingled emotions of the massed listeners. His absorption in this discovery, however, puts him into danger, for his resulting failure to follow the forms of worship, plus the deliberate action of the priest upon this psi field, turns this massed emotion against him. He finds that it precludes reason, he must also fight panic within himself, and he must discover the uses of caution. Although he feels himself on the brink of greater understanding, the meaning is not yet clear; nevertheless, he has reached the point where he can declare himself a graduate of the ordeal. Even so, he must yet seek out the Abbod, both because of his mission for I-A and because his learning is not yet complete.

In finding the Abbod, his mind works as an I-A agent's mind should work, as demonstrated on Hamal; however, this time the I-A interpretations are not valid, for the Abbod is alone and unprotected, except by his own force of personality and knowledge. In this meeting, Orne is brought to acknowledge that a primary purpose of the ordeals has been to bring him knowledge which he lacked. Another purpose, which he acknowledges, is to develop a discipline in the use of his awesome powers. Finally, he removes himself to a point where he can observe the universe, where he finds that the motive of life is life itself and that more danger is involved in trying to suppress any of the infinite possibilities than is any of those possibilities themselves. Through this revelation, he comes to understand why the priests are opposing the I-A, and allows the I-A to be eliminated as a separate agency and to become a part of R&R. On the other hand, having found through personal experience that R&R is error-prone, he also makes sure that former I-A agents are given meaningful places within it, thus insuring that the past errors of both groups are modified. Once this has been accomplished, he leaves on his honeymoon with Diana Bullone.

Thus, Lewis Orne's development follows the traditional pattern of the development of the hero. He moves from an unusual birth (a mother consciously determining the sex of the child at conception), to setting out upon a quest (joining R&R and later I-A to bring back together an empire shattered by war), through a series of tests designed to determine his qualifications and provide him with various kinds of knowledge and understanding, to recognition of his capabilities and assumption of his role, to using his powers for the good of the people and the empire, and to marriage with a princess (Diana Bullone is, after all, the daughter of the highest official of the Galactic Empire). His "death" and rebirth, both physically and spiritually, the fact that he has a number of guides and helpers, and the fact that a great deal of the knowledge that he gains is self-knowledge are all consistent with the initiation of the hero. Even the transition of the hero from mortal man to literal god can be found in many heroic adventures.

Closely related to Orne's development as a hero-god is the growth of his understanding of war and violence; each stage of his development toward godhood also marks an increased understanding of these complex forces. For example, when he is on Hamal, his first thoughts are of justifying himself for notifying I-A and of preventing the possible outbreak of a war, such as the one which destroyed the old empire. Before he leaves the planet, however, he recognizes the nasty things an occupation force does to a place in the name of preventing war; he also wishes there were some other way of preventing possible military excursions, thinking that perhaps a new religion would help people find a better balance in their lives. In the episode on Gienah, the first impulse of Stetson and others is to totally destroy the planet; one of the forces which drives Orne in his contact with the natives is a desire to avoid such a course. In addition, throughout this mission, his sympathies lie with the natives, and he questions the right of frightened humans to determine the destruction of any intelligent beings. Because of these feelings, he finds ways to prevent the expression of hostile feelings on both sides and finds a means of accommodation; although he does not like the idea of occupation, he does find it better than annihilation. Finally, the idea of the hoe and the handle occurs to him for the first time while he is on Gienah; this would be one means of preventing war, for each group would be dependent on the others, with something to lose if another is destroyed; it would also lessen the number of things that might motivate a war. By the time Orne has been wounded in the Sheleb Incident, he has brought Stetson to the point that he admits that for every good thing brought about by an occupation force, an evil occurs, leaving the people demoralized and shattered. However, at this point, both of them still seem to think of war simply in terms of evil and in terms of preventing it; neither of them has really examined their premises.

While he is in the crechepod, Orne does begin to examine these premises and to look at the nature of war and of the universe. He wonders, for example, about whether man might not be trapped within his own invention, unable to break free. He wonders about the ways in which the universe influences man without his knowledge. He wonders about the right of I-A to mediate the affairs of all sentient life. And he comes to the realization that repressing a thing, instead of eliminating it, only makes it the stronger, giving impetus to an equal thrust in the opposite direction. This is a point for which Stetson has the words but not the understanding; he points out during his investigation of Hamal that those who are really committed to peace have developed an entire social dynamic in which the concept of peace as it is usually known does not even occur—nor does the concept of war. Thus, the more we talk about peace, the more prominent its opposite becomes. Nevertheless, he does not apply these words to the I-A and its activities.

In view of the fairly recent past history of the Galactic League, some of the attitudes shown by the I-A may be reasonable and originated from good motivations. That is, some centuries before, the entire civilization was shattered by the Rim Wars, fought primarily between the old Marakian League and the Nathians. Planets that were once a part of a whole are still being re-found at the time of the story; in fact, finding them again and bringing them back into the Galactic League is and has been the function of R&R, just as preventing another outbreak of that kind of war has been the function of I-A. As Orne suggests while he is in the crechepod, they are, in a sense, trying to reshape the past, or at the very least allowing the hand of the past to guide the future. This has led to the lack of re-examination of premises noted earlier. The turning point away from this action comes with Lewis Orne's realizations in the crechepod.

Both the grip of past history and the change of direction can be seen in the conspiracy which is uncovered in the home of High Commissioner Bullone. Polly Bullone, her daughters, Lewis's mother and sisters, and the wives and daughters of many government officials are Nathians, as is Lewis Orne himself. The primary thing about the Nathians 500 years after the Rim Wars is that they are a group of women who can control the sex of their offspring and who are extremely astute political scientists; furthermore, they have infiltrated the societies rebuilding after the war and have mixed their blood thoroughly with the rest of the galactic society. However, the name Nathian is enough to set many people into a panic, including Stetson and his superiors; their immediate reaction is to wipe them out, without thinking about the possibilitity of starting another war in the process, which may be the best reason for eliminating I-A as an independent arm of the government.

Lewis Orne effects the compromise which recognizes that the Nathians must provide good government to achieve their ends and eliminates the possibility of total Nathian take-over of the entire government. In doing so he uses the principle of the hoe and the handle; the Nathians make the blade by choosing their candidates and grooming them as they have in the past, while Stetson, Orne, Admiral Spencer, and others will have veto power, in addition to limiting Nathian candidates to only half of the high offices. The final steps in this process, and the completion of this thematic thread, come when Lewis Orne steps outside of time and comes to understand that in an infinite system all things must be possible, that things change; all of the other things that he has learned through his tests and ordeals also contribute to this conclusion. To bring about this possibility, he allows the dissolution of I-A to be accomplished through the political processes. However, to recognize war as one of the possibilities that must be open and as one of the means of accomplishing change does not mean that war is a desirable state or that he feels it should be allowed to start by accident or by stupidity. To prevent this, he makes sure that the former I-A agents are scattered throughout the ranks of R&R, with substantial voice in what happens. Finally, there is some suggestion that he might work to bring about a social dynamic which is peaceful, which helps people, as individuals and as planetary populations, to find a balance in which they can comfortably fit, thus reducing the impetus and the need for war.

To simplify greatly, one of the primary points made through this thematic thread is that neither war nor peace can be seen as absolutely good or absolutely evil. Another point stressed is that imposed and enforced peace may indeed be a surer way to create war. However, the novel postulates other means of avoiding war, though vaguely. One suggestion is the founding of a religion which would help find an equilibrium which would reduce their need to war on others and to accept their place in the larger scheme of things. Another suggestion involves finding ways to avoid putting populations in positions where they need to justify themselves or where they have cause to feel self-righteous. Nevertheless, without recognizing any particular goodness in war, the novel thematically insists that it must be a possibility and that it not be judged simplistically from either direction.

Another theme which receives consistent attention throughout the novel deals with religion. Like everything else in the book, it is closely related to Lewis Orne's development into godhood, but it is treated somewhat more vaguely than the theme of his development or the theme of war. It would seem that the point from which Herbert makes his departure along these lines is the idea that if there were no god, man would create one; although mythology often deals with men who become gods, in this case Herbert proceeds rather more literally in these matters. For that matter, there is ample evidence in the novel that man has created, not simply one god, but many; in fact, the creation of a god has been reduced to a science, although that science involves only the knowledge of setting certain forces in motion without knowledge of what might happen once those forces have been set in motion. Perhaps one of the most interesting points made in the novel is the definition of a god as a psi focus. As Orne discovers in the test of ceremony and dogma, the mingled emotions of a mass of people do create a psi field that has a focus and that can be manipulated; the creation of a god would then seem to involve creating something which such a psi field would naturally focus on. There are a number of instances where a power, for want of a better term, is felt to be emanating from Lewis Orne; for example, Stetson seems strongly attached to and influenced by him and, too, Abbod Halmyrach prays to him. Another major aspect of the theme is the fact that there is an ecumenical peace so complete that religious strife has been reduced to nothing and that *all* the religions in the known universe have their center on a single planet, with a total mingling of functions. Another interesting element in this theme is the fact that psi and religion are presented as simply two different ways of explaining the same thing in many instances; what the Psi Branch of I-A might call the workings of a psi focus, the religious would call a miracle, even though both were talking about exactly the same event. Thus, the training involved on Amel is both religious and psi oriented; to put it another way, psi is used to further religious training, while religious training is always involved in psi training. Finally, many of the things that Lewis Orne learns about himself, about war, and about the nature of the universe, which have already been discussed in a slightly different context, are also applicable to the theme of religion. Although religion is an important element in this book, it is more closely involved in the other elements, making it difficult to derive any separable statements about it; it acts more as an agency through which other elements are more clearly and completely seen than as a separate theme in its own right.

In many ways *The Godmakers* is similar to *Dune* and could be said to portray a point in the history of humankind mid-way between the present and the time of *Dune*. One particularly noticeable point of similarity is the use of Arbs or Arybs as the basis of the Nathians, just as the Fremen are descended of apparently Arab stock. In addition, the Nathian women can almost be seen as the forerunners of the Bene Gesserit, with their tight organization, their political manipulation, their ability to determine the sex of their offspring, and the dominance of daughters among them. The major themes are also similar, though *The Godmakers* treats these themes from a different perspective and in a different way; in the sense that the treatment of these elements is simpler and more direct in *The Godmakers* than in *Dune*, this novel might well be profitably read before moving into the complex world of *Dune*.

UNDER PRESSURE
1956

Formerly titled *The Dragon in the Sea, Under Pressure* is Frank Herbert's first novel. For a first novel, it is fine science fiction, and it shows the signs of the detail and complexity that later won Herbert the Nebula and Hugo Awards for *Dune*. The story-line follows four men in a submarine as they leave from a "secret" base in the United States, meet a series of crises on their way to pirate undersea oil from the Eastern Powers, accomplish their goal, and return home after overcoming further crises. Weaving through and around this story sequence are three basic areas of exploration: 1.) the nature and workings of a submarine, only slightly extrapolated from current knowledge and models; 2.) the nature and workings of a society at war and in which such piracy is necessary; and 3.) the psychological adaptations which human beings make, both to the conditions in a submarine and to the larger social conditions.

In the area of submarine technology and the undersea world, *Under Pressure* is reminiscent of Jules Verne's *20,000 Leagues under the Sea*. In both novels, there is a great deal of interest in how a submarine works; in both cases, the technical explanations are based on a careful extrapolation from the best and most recent scientific information available to the authors. Furthermore, both writers provide information about the world in which the submarine exists, although Verne is particularly interested in undersea fauna and flora, whereas Herbert concentrates more on undersea geography. There is, however, a difference of emphasis between these two novels, for Herbert places much more emphasis on the technological aspects, while Verne is far more fascinated by the world outside the submarine; to a large extent, of course, those elements which Herbert emphasizes are the ones which are necessary to the story-line or which reinforce the other areas of exploration. For example, since the submarine *Fenian Ram;* in the course of its journey, must evade enemy submarines, the capabilities of the *Ram* for doing so are important, as are any features of the sea and its floor that the crew could utilize to hide or to escape detection. In addition, since the interior of the submarine is the primary environment in which the crew must live, adapt, and interact, with the sea outside important but secondary, it is reasonable and necessary for the interior technology to be stressed more fully in the novel. As a matter of comparison, it would seem that Verne created his submarine, chose his characters, and arranged his story-line for the primary purpose of exploring the world under the sea, which accounts for many of the differences between *20,000 Leagues under the Sea* and *Under Pressure.*

The general society in which this adventure story takes place is rather vague, but the elements that are provided are essential to the story and to the theme of psychological adaptation. The first main point about this society is the fact that it has been at war for sixteen years. Perhaps one of the important aspects that is implied but not specified is the fact that atomic weapons have been used, but not in an all-out manner; Britain has been wiped out, and the sea in that area is extremely radioactive, but there is no indication that American or Russian—or even any other targets besides Britain—have been bombarded with atomic warheads. The only possible exception to this is the Corpus Christi crater, but the indications are that this was caused by a sabotaged submarine without atomic weapons. Also interesting is the fact that the combatants are not particularly specified; the enemy is simply known as the EP (Eastern Powers), with only Russia identified as a member. It may also be assumed that the United States has allies, though they are unnamed. Finally, it would seem that this war between unnamed forces lies somewhere between a cold war and a shooting war. There is a good deal of the propaganda and spy work associated with the cold war and some of the shooting associated with a hot war, but the main thrust of the war activity seems to be various kinds of sabotage.

The second major aspect of this society, and an almost inevitable consequence of the first point, is that Security has become one of the most powerful of government agencies, and that fear and distrust are commonplace on all levels of life. The training that Ramsey undergoes is kept extremely secret; his room is continuously monitored, and his wife is allowed only limited visits. The crew of the *Fenian Ram* is checked over intensively just before the journey—again—and the entire submarine is gone over several times. The government attempts to keep its oil-pirating secret and pretends that the number and location of its submarine bases are. However, this fear and distrust, carried to the extreme that they are carried, backfires on occasion. In the first place, it tends to make the crews of the submarines more nervous and more suspicious of one another in a crisis; coupled with the drawn-out nature of the war and the failure of the twenty previous missions, this creates an extremely low morale among these crews. Equally important is the fact that even if a sleeper—an agent who does not function for many years—wanted to turn himself in, as Garcia did, he does not dare to do so; the fear of turning himself in is greater than his fear of prison camp or death.

It should also be noted that the Bureau of Psychology—BuPsych or BP—has also gained a great deal of power in the government. It seems to be an independent agency, but it cooperates fully with Security and with the administrative branch in the course of the novel. It seems quite clear that the purpose of the Bureau of Psychology is two-fold: 1.) to help with the mental health of people involved in the war effort, such as the crews of the subtugs; and 2.) to find ways to keep the country, as a whole, supporting the war. However, its director, Dr. Richmond Oberhausen, has other designs, manipulating things so that by the end of the war, Security will be under the control of BuPsych; from his control at the beginning of the novel, it seems quite likely that he can succeed with this plan. This, of course, is both hopeful and frightening. It is hopeful because it can effectively nullify the power and the machinations of Security. It is frightening because it opens the possibility of wholesale manipulation of a nation by a small group of people; while there is no doubt that this could be beneficial, so much depends on the good will and the knowledge of a very few people.

All of these things, however, are most important as the background against which the psychological adaptations of the crew of the *Fenian Ram,* and the psychological development of Ensign "Long John" Ramsey in particular, are explored. At the beginning of the novel, Ramsey is described as tall, round-faced, and soft-looking (though he isn't); he has also been an Ensign much longer than normal, a fact which Dr. Oberhausen explains as due to the jealousy of the service branches for having kept his top men out of uniform. He has been chosen for this job because of his dual qualifications: he is both an excellent psychologist and an excellent amateur in electronics. He also has the advantage of being able to improvise and to devise gadgets, or modify existing ones, to meet emergencies. However, as can be seen during his training session and through his attitudes toward the other three crew members, and as Garcia points out explicitly toward the end of the novel, he tends to exhibit a know-it-all attitude. This is more apparent than real, for even at the beginning of the novel, he is shown to have frequent self-doubts. Thus, in part, this attitude seems to be a defense mechanism to conceal his self-doubts; in part, it is also due to his profession and to the fact that, especially in the context of this society and novel, psychologists believe that they have plumbed the secrets of human motivation and thus can manipulate them in any way desired (one clear example of this is the meeting at the beginning of the book, and it can also be seen in the way that Ramsey strives to break Sparrow's control, especially at the end of the novel). To a large extent, this "professional attitude" forms the basis for the learning process that Ramsey undergoes and the background against which it can be seen and measured.

One of the things that Ramsey learns on this voyage under the sea is that psychologists in general and he in particular do not have all the answers about the human mind and the ways in which it adapts to various situations. Closely related to this is the fact that psychologists are not the only people capable of analyzing themselves and their situations and coming up with answers which shed light on a problem and which produce a workable solution or course of action. Both aspects of this bit of learning manifest themselves early in the voyage, when Captain Sparrow suggests that the underground base is like a womb and the marine tunnel like a birth canal; Ramsey is startled that Sparrow has come up with this, and he feels that it should have originated with BuPsych and is chagrined that it didn't. Even so, he doesn't realize the full implications of this analogy and the ways in which it bears on the problem of the breakdown of the subtug crews until the end of the novel; furthermore, he must go into a catatonic withdrawal before he can force himself to realize and face these implications. In the process, of course, he learns something about himself that he didn't know before. Both aspects of this learning also manifest themselves when Ramsey learns that Sparrow has known for some time that his particular adaptation to the kind of life he must lead is a mechanical functioning and an identification with his submarine. As they discuss this, it is clear that Sparrow has pondered this and, also, the nature of sanity; he points out to Ramsey that adaptation to situations and to various threats to survival are, by definition, insane because sanity is defined by a context with minimal threat to survival and that sanity is the ability to understand what is required in different situations. It is this conversation, or something within it, that sends Ramsey into catatonic withdrawal. When he comes out of it, however, he has the answers — or some of them — to the problem he was sent to solve. Using Sparrow's birth canal analogy as a starting point, he suggests that it works both ways, sending the crews into an environment where the requirements are very different whichever way they go. He also points out the relationship between the sea and amniotic fluid, between life in the submarine and in the womb; although there are many dangers under the sea, the sea lulls the unconscious, and life in the submarine creates all the emotional ties and rivalries of siblings among the crew members, thus making the shock of returning to land equivalent to the shock of birth. It has been the failure to make the full circle desirable that has been partially responsible for the breakdown of the crews (another part seems to be the manipulations of Security and the never-endingness of the war). In the course of learning this, Ramsey also comes to a better understanding of himself and of his psychological needs. Perhaps the most basic of these understandings is that he needs and desires a father-figure, someone who is strong and knowledgeable. He also discovers that he wants very much to be accepted as part of a group and to feel close ties with other human beings but that, ironically, his defense mechanisms prevent this closeness. By the end of the novel, then, Ramsey seems to be a more complete human being and more at ease with himself. He has come to realize the limitations of psychology and the flaws in his earlier attitudes toward it. Thus, a major thrust of *Under Pressure* is the maturation process Ramsey undergoes.

Under Pressure is a relatively complex novel, blending many details of these three major threads to make an exciting adventure story which also has a great deal to say about man and his adaptations to his environment. Although the primary focus of this exploration of man's adaptations is on Johnny Ramsey, it is important to remember that Sparrow, Les Bonnett, and Joe Garcia also show other adaptations, other ways of handling the pressures which they face, even though these have not been explored here. Because the novel provides so much information about the technology involved and because the exploration of human reactions concerns the relation between man and his machines as they mediate between him and his environment, *Under Pressure* is a good, solid blend of extrapolative hard science fiction and extrapolative soft science fiction; while there is very little in the novel that we do not now know, the way in which the elements are combined sheds new light on them all.

DESTINATION: VOID
1966

In some ways, it seems incredible to think that *Destination: Void* was written shortly after *Dune;* its style and its handling of the subject matter seem to indicate that it was written earlier and published after *Dune* had been published. However, *Destination: Void* does share with *Dune* an interest in human consciousness, its nature and its limits, although this is the primary—the only—focus of *Destination: Void,* whereas it is simply a part of *Dune.* It is only fair to point out that, in spite of its weaknesses, this novel does raise a number of interesting points and questions, and the process of building an artificial, or man-made, consciousness does have its interest.

It can be said that the nature of consciousness is explored from two directions in this novel, through the personal interactions of the characters and through the building of the Ox, also involving the concepts which guide their construction activities; these two directions do, of course, converge in the telling of the story. The interactions between the four members of the crew are particularly interesting because of what they show about the society which sent them on this mission and about its attitudes toward human beings. In the first place, there are 3,006 humans aboard the ship *Earthling* heading, supposedly, toward Tau Ceti to settle one of its planets; of this number, six are an umbilicus crew to take the ship out of the solar system, after which they would join the others in hibernation. Even while they are awake, but especially after they go into hibernation, the functioning of the ship is the responsibility of the Organic Mental Core (OMC), which is a human brain taken from a child who would otherwise have had no chance to live and exclusively trained for the job of running the ship. Although it is obvious which course this society took in this matter, the question of the morality of the choice is briefly raised and both sides indicated, but the reader is left to his own judgment in the matter; in brief, it is a question of the fact of preserving life versus the quality of living that life is preserved for. This is complicated by the fact that by the time the *Eqrthling* is just over a quarter of the way across the solar system, its OMC *and* its two back-ups have gone insane, each in a shorter time than it took the one before it; not only do they go insane, however, but it also appears that Moonbase was aware that this might happen, for it did, after all, send three of them. It is interested to note that, in semi-opposition to the OMCs, the colonists and the umbilicus crew are Doppelgangers, grown from cells of people remaining back on Earth; in addition, these cells were taken from people who were brilliant but in some way criminal. The umbilicus crew, and its back-ups, are the best men available, chosen for their particular abilities but also because of the potential relationships between them; although it is never said, it would almost seem that personality types were chosen and then trained for the jobs that must be done. Thus, Raja Flattery is the psychiatrist-chaplain, with a smattering of knowledge in other areas; this combination seems to have been chosen for three reasons: to have someone capable of creatively handling the tensions of the crew, to provide psychological information when it is needed for the project, and to goad John Bickel along the paths he needs to go. Flattery does these quite well, but he also reveals the battle in the human mind between faith and skepticism, as well as showing a definite streak of mysticism. In addition, it is he who is the prime enunciator of the "Frankenstein fear," the fear of moving into areas man should stay out of, though each of the four echoes this at some time; in doing so, he seems to be the spokesman for the Control Center on Moonbase, who in turn seems to speak for the mass of mankind, then and now. Prudence Weygand is trained in medicine, ecology, and computer math, all of which are valuable in the project, as is her facility with tools; she is also extremely compassionate, but that is linked with her sex drive, which must be suppressed. Like Flattery, she has been primed to goad Bickel when necessary, but she also serves the same function for Flattery, mocking him when he becomes too pompous, and keeping him alert. John Bickel is the focal point of the group; he is aggressive, creative, brilliant, subtle, and explosive. If the mission is to have any success at all, it is Bickel who will both lead the way and make it happen. The goading that Raj and Prue do is partly to push him in particular directions, and partly to put obstacles in his way so that he will overcome them in frustration. It is interesting that the society feels the need to create a situation like this; it means either that they have a precise knowledge of how people work best or it means they care only for results, no matter what it takes to achieve them. In this company, Gerrill Timberlake is almost a nonentity; he is the life-systems engineer and is also very capable in electronics. Although Bickel is not primed in the same way Flattery and Weygand are, he nevertheless serves as a goad to Timberlake, who does very fine work under Bickel's direction and even develops new ideas and directions.

In a way similar to this psychological manipulation of the personal interactions of the crew, so Moonbase Control has manipulated their entire life aboard the *Earthling*. That is, they have built in programmed emergencies to keep the crew alert, and they have withheld a great deal of information from the crew. For example, they have provided three OMCs, but have given the crew no indications of the possibility that an OMC might break down and no code for reporting such an event. It is postulated in the book that this breakdown is known and that its possibility (probability) is exploited to force the crew into a situation where they must produce or die, all of which speaks of a rather cold-blooded, but practical, approach to the matter. Although there are many other matters which Moonbase Control has concealed from the crew, two of them are particularly worth mentioning. First, they deliberately keep Bickel from pursuing his ideas while he is in training, apparently to make sure that he uses them on the ship. Second, they do not show the full linkage system in the computer in the schematics, presumably because they know that the full computer network is necessary for a result and that some part of the crew would prevent such a tie-in if it were to be done as part of an experiment. In addition to all this, the voyage of the *Earthling* has been arranged so that the ship can never return to Earth. The management involved does not present a very pretty picture of a society; nevertheless, it does achieve results, although they are not precisely the ones desired.

The point of the entire project, and of all the manipulation undertaken by Moonbase Control, is the creation of an artificial consciousness that is not inimical to mankind and that can in some way be controlled by man. These last two conditions are built in because several earlier attempts turned apparently rogue, killing people and disappearing; it is for this reason that this crew is sent far into space and that dual destruct mechanisms are built into the ship. All of the manipulations discussed earlier are designed to point people toward creation of this artificial consciousness, to make it *necessary* for them to do so if they are to survive. In their pursuit of this goal, several interesting points about consciousness are made.

Perhaps the most interesting, and most basic, idea that is advanced is the field theory idea of consciousness. There are three elements necessary to the field theory: a person who perceives something, the object he perceives, and the relationship between the person and the object; it is this relationship which, according to the novel, is primarily responsible for the whole being greater than the sum of its parts, for the interaction is contained in neither of the parts separately. In fact, however, the field theory implies even more than this because, through memory, consciousness includes relationships between many sets of person-object interactions through many levels. Beyond this, however, introspection, sensing, feeling, and thinking are ruled out as being physiological functions, and awareness as such is declared to be insufficient. It is interesting to note that, in the midst of their attempts to define consciousness, Bickel points out that even if something cannot be defined, it can be reproduced; while his specific reference is to consciousness, this idea has application across the field of science. However, they do know a number of things about consciousness and field theory that they do incorporate into their construct. For example, they suggest that a certain amount of complexity in the network of connections in the field is necessary before consciousness can be achieved. In fact, the point is made that, relatively speaking, human beings do not have sufficient complexity to be fully aware; but it is possible to build something with enough complexity to handle much more data and many more relationships. Nevertheless, the flow of sensory data is so great that some means of sorting it all out is necessary. First of all, then, they postulate a threshhold effect, a tuning in of data that is in some way significant or relevant or related to previous data; this may be more or less selective, depending on circumstances at any given time. In fact, the ability to select data is a basic element in their definition of consciousness. Second, they postulate the idea that, even with the threshhold effect, a stepping-down process must take place. That is, masses of sensory data are brought into the system and, through a series of steps, are brought down to fewer and fewer discrete signals until we perceive an image. In this process, matching data reinforce each other while the weaker or non-matching data are eliminated or made secondary; however, sufficient discrimination remains so that similarity or dissimilarity to previous experience can be judged. Third, they postulate that consciousness needs a goal, something to give direction to its processes, and that it needs sensory, emotional, and mental data to respond to and to regulate. The sensory and mental responses are not particularly difficult to build into their construct, but building an emotional response into a technological device poses some problems; Bickel proposes the black box-white box transfer effect and finally, in effect, hooks himself into the system and transfers his experiences and his approaches to them into it. An unexpected side effect that the experiential and emotional indices of all the crew, awake or in hibernation, are also experienced by their construct. Fourth, they recognize that synergy must occur, that there must be some means for unconscious energy transfer from one area to another. Finally, implicit in all this is the idea that consciousness cannot be determined, that free will is necessary before consciousness can arise. In addition to these factors that they consciously develop, there are two points which they do not consider but which are necessary if consciousness is achieved. The first is provided, although they have not concluded it; that is, before consciousness can be achieved, some kind of symbol manipulator is essential. This is provided by the AAT, the Accept-And-Translate board for taking messages from Earth and sending them back. The second element that is accidentally provided is the destruct mechanism, armed when Moonbase Control orders the mission totally aborted; thus, the possibility of an ending is provided, as is a background against which life can be measured and evaluated. By building these elements into their construct, they do create consciousness, but one which has far more awareness, far more data, and far more ability to see relationships than mankind; the novel ends with this consciousness demanding worship.

Two flaws of *Destination: Void* are those usually involved in gadget science fiction. When the emphasis is on building a device and on the ideas involved in it, story and character values tend to fall by the wayside. Thus, although we learn a number of things about the characters, these are related totally to their function in the project, and they come across as rather lifeless. Furthermore, since the events of the story are nearly all steps in the creation of the artificial consciousness, if the reader is not excited about this concept, he has nothing else to hold onto. However, the ideas and themes with which he works, although more could have been done with them, are not seriously flawed. We do, for example, learn quite a bit about the society which frames the particular situation in the novel. Furthermore, although not all schools of psychological thought would agree, the points which he makes about consciousness would be accepted as valid by others. Thus, if the reader is interested in these things, he will very likely derive some measure of enjoyment from this book.

THE EYES OF HEISENBERG
1966

The Eyes of Heisenberg is not one of Herbert's better novels, lacking the depth, detail, and suggestiveness of such novels as *Dune* or even *The Godmakers*. Nevertheless, it is an easy-reading and rather interesting exploration of two themes, immortality and the centralization of power. These themes are intertwined thoroughly, for the Optimen who hold the power — absolute power — in this society are potentially immortal. There is, however, one major weakness in their potential for immortality, for to achieve it, they must lead quiet, stable lives and they must use a variety of drugs to maintain a rather precise hormonal and enzymic balance. It is on this weakness that the rebellion focuses its strategy, for only through disrupting this balance can they hope to upset the power structure enough to gain their own ends. Finally, in the course of the exploration of these two themes, we also find out a great deal about the society in which the story takes place; in fact, this may well be the most interesting aspect of the novel.

Perhaps the most basic fact of this society is genetic engineering. As though to emphasize this, the first three chapters of the novel are devoted to a description of the tailoring of a human embryo; these chapters also introduce most of the main characters — Harvey and Lizbeth Durant, Dr. Vyaslav Potter, and Dr. Thei Svengaard. To some extent, this tailoring produces an endless circle; in the process, the ability to reproduce without medical and technological assistance has been almost totally lost, and many within the population, including all of the Optimen, are sterile, incapable of reproducing their own kind in any way. It is for this reason that the Durant embryo becomes so important, for by some unknown means it becomes self-viable and, in the process, resistant to manipulation by the gene surgeons. To the Optimen, this embryo is important because it will be beyond their control; it will be resistant to the contraceptive gas they put into the air, it will not need to rely on their permission to breed, and its hormonal balance will be natural so that it will not have need of the medical assistance all others need — all of which are means the Optimen use to control the general population. (The Optimen are set apart from the rest of the population by two factors: greater intelligence and, more important, greater ability to balance the Life Force through delicately adjusted enzyme intake, which allows virtual immortality.) This embryo is also important to the Parents' Underground and to the Cyborgs because of its self-viability and its resistance to the means of control; however, whereas the Optimen wish to destroy the embryo because of the threat that it will pose, the Parents' Underground and the Cyborgs wish to preserve it for that same reason. There is, though, a major difference in the ultimate ends the Cyborgs and the Parents' Underground wish to achieve. The Underground simply wants to be free of the control that the Optimen have over them, to be able to live their lives as they choose. The Cyborgs, on the other hand, hope to replace the Optimen; they are the results of abandoned experiments by Optimen, which increases the animosity between the two groups, and they espouse bionic change of humans — grafting electronic tools onto and into the human body — rather than biological manipulation of embryos, which indicates deep philosophical differences between them. The struggle, in fact, is primarily between the Optimen and the Cyborgs, for they both have access to knowledge and technological devices that mere humans are denied; the humans are the pawns of the other groups, manipulated by both until near the very end.

In planning their second attempt to gain power — there had been a war fought some time earlier between Cyborgs and Optimen — the Cyborgs used the Durant embryo as a focal point. First, they switch another embryo for the Durants'. Then they make sure that the Optimen are aware of their escape from Seatac Megalopolis; most obvious is the way that Potter's guide (he is to implant the embryo in its mother) steps out in the open and fires against the weapons of the Optimen, thus forcing them to give up or fight back. This strategy is carefully chosen, for the virtual immortality (the first is 80,000 years old and still going) of the Optimen is dependent on enzyme prescriptions to keep their physical systems in balance; for these prescriptions to work, however, their environment must be kept stable and their emotions must be kept in check. Thus, the strategy is to get the Optimen excited, to force them out of the patterns of response they have devised. It is most effective, for the struggle gradually involves nearly all the Optimen, as greater violence is used; they become intensely involved emotionally, which sends their physical balance oscillating wildly. With the Cyborg Glisson in the Optimen stronghold, though under restraint, this is precisely what the Cyborgs had been aiming toward. Unfortunately, in their arrogance, they made several errors. First, they did not consider the possibility that the humans would distrust and reject them — as they do the Optimen. Second, they did not consider the possible effect of the presence of Dr. Thei Svengaard in the group at Central; he is present mostly by accident, but he does not accept the Cyborg view of the Optimen or even that of the Parents' Underground. Third, they did not consider an alternative to their plan possible, or that the humans might be capable of developing such an alternative. However, Svengaard does come up with an alternative, emplanting embryos in all Optimen — and all mere humans — and retarding their development, thus providing a natural means of balancing and secreting the enzymes the body needs to function. Through this means, the Optimen will be able to have an extremely long life, though they will not be immortal, and they will be able to feel emotion and to experience many things previously denied them. In addition, by proposing this, Svengaard wins many concessions for the humans. The only real losers seem to be the Cyborgs, who remain in very much the same position they started from.

The principal cause of the upheaval in this society, aside from the jealousy of the Cyborgs and their desire for power and revenge, is the complex of attitudes held by the Optimen as a result of their virtual immortality. Perhaps most telling within this complex is their refusal to admit the possibility of death; it is as though they believe that by not speaking of death or disease, by using euphemisms for anything related to death and disease, they can ignore them and the reality of death and disease will cease to be. In fact, the progress of the Optimen toward near disintegration is clearly marked by their increasing use of words related to these two facets of ordinary life, as well as by their exhilaration at the violence going on about them. Probably equally, or even more, important in provoking rebellion is the fear of change exhibited in many ways by the Optimen. They actively work, through their human agents and their machines, to control what happens in the world outside of Central, allowing nothing that would disturb life as they know it. In the process, they create a regimented police state based on fear that is masked by worship. It is also suggested that the Optimen have several "political factions," from Actionists to Esthetes; it is just as clearly indicated that these are phases the Optimen go through as they grow older and that the progression is from greater activity and greater interest in a variety of things toward less activity and interest. These, as well as other factors, point to the idea that although they are physically alive the Optimen are not really alive, are not using their lives for anything worthwhile other than simply staying alive. The point is, as Svengaard suggests, that they are adolescents who have never grown up emotionally; in not facing death and in not facing change, they have not allowed themselves to become adults, to experience life, and to use their lives meaningfully. Thus, immortality, or even extremely long life, is seen to have distinct disadvantages if not used properly; however, because the ending of the novel points this society in a different direction, there is the strong suggestion that it may also have many advantages if approached maturely.

The title of *The Eyes of Heisenberg* refers to the Heisenberg principle, which suggests that indeterminacy increases as a system becomes more determined. Thus, as the Optimen try to control their environment more and more, they become less able to do so because the number of actions and events they cannot control also increases. On one level, then, this is the significance of the novel. On another level, its significance lies in the exploration of age and maturity and of the uses of life. Through these explorations, and throughout them, Herbert creates a potential future society. Although this may not be one of Herbert's better books, it is *not* bad science fiction, for it tells an interesting story, creates a consistent world, and holds out for the reader's consideration several themes of no little pertinence.

THE GREEN BRAIN

1966

Although Frank Herbert has been consistently concerned with ecology on its various levels, *The Green Brain* is the novel which focuses most directly and most single-mindedly on the theme of ecological destruction. It is also the novel which makes the most apparent demands on the reader's credulity, with its living brain tended by insects and its clusters of insects which can link themselves together in such a way as to form a passable imitation of a man; however, these two assumptions are plot devices rather than central assumptions that must be accepted for the novel to make sense. Once they are provisionally accepted, they facilitate matters considerably without really changing the basic situation. Although they do tend to get in the way at times, the novel is nevertheless pertinent and worth the time spent in reading it.

The novel is set in South America, in Brazil. Under the auspices of the International Ecological Organization (IEO), a massive effort is being made to eliminate all forms of insect life, section by section, apparently until the entire continent is "clean"; the plan is then to introduce mutated bees to serve the necessary functions, such as cross fertilization. The regional director of IEO is Dr. Travis Huntington Chen-Lhu; he has been assigned to this effort because China has completed its realignment of insects. Some very interesting points are brought up in the first part of the book, within the first forty-two pages. First, it is shown that the insects are rapidly and radically mutating to meet the severe threat to their survival; one of these survival mutations is the clustering of insects to imitate a man, another is increase in size by some of the insects, and a third is immunity to the poisons which the bandeirantes (the Brazilian insect exterminators) use against them. The basis of this point is, of course, quite well established: we have already seen the need to continue to develop new poisons in fairly rapid succession to keep up with the adaptations of insects to poisons which once were successful against them; with their short life-spans and the overwhelming tendency for survival mutations to breed true, it does not take the insect world long to meet any particular threat to its survival. However, although mutation is a well-known phenomenon, the particular mutations suggested here seem more for the purpose of dramatizing an extreme situation rather than aiming toward full realism. A second point that has some interest is the fact that a number of countries, including the United States and Canada, are holding out against this elimination of insects; that this is so makes China's dual attitude all the more significant: on the one hand, they are leading the fight against the insects, but on the other hand, they will allow no one to visit their country to see their results, achieved over a twenty-year period. Their excuse for keeping others out is the years they spent dominated by foreign imperialists; however, we later come to learn that the real reason for both aspects of their dual position is the failure of their program, the fact that the land has gone sterile and that the mutated bees have been insufficient. Thus, they do not want the world to know of their failure, and there will be an element of saving face if others also fail. Throughout the novel, Dr. Chen-Lhu seeks to set up Johnny Martinho, one of the more important leaders of a bandeirante group, as a scapegoat if the program of realignment fails in either way; he will be a scapegoat particularly if there is a failure in eliminating the insects, but Chen-Lhu is also setting up someone to take the blame if the Brazilian result is the same as China's. A third point of interest is the fact that Johnny Martinho, who has been a leader from the first in this realignment of insects, is also one of the leaders in questioning the wisdom of continuing this course of action. He and other bandeirantes have seen much more of the mutated forms of insects than they care to; those that are seen in the city early in the novel are only one example. However, it is particularly convenient for Chen-Lhu and others to foster rumors that the bandeirantes are responsible for these mutations, developing them in secret laboratories; in fact, Chen-Lhu openly repeats the accusation to Johnny Martinho and others when the mutated insect is seen at the plaza, suggesting either that they have created such mutations or that they have arranged for some kind of masquerade to fool the people. Clearly, the climate of opinion is carefully prepared, for when the mutated insects have appeared, the people become a mob directed at the bandeirantes.

Thus, the lines of conflict are drawn early in the novel. The overlying conflict is between men and insects; this is a two-way conflict, with man trying to destroy the insects, and the insects trying in a variety of ways to survive and to make some kind of contact with humans so that the destruction might be stopped. It is at this later point that the brain in the cave in the forest becomes important, for it is this brain that coordinates the activities of the insects and gives a conscious direction to their survival patterns. Furthermore, the brain seeks to find some mutual accommodation with humans, to find a few humans who can be made to see the mistake of destroying the insects and then return to civilization to persuade others; throughout the musings of the brain and the activities of the insects directed by it, the emphasis is on survival and defense, with only enough offensive power displayed to bring about the necessary results of bringing humans to the brain. Thematically, there is a strong suggestion that the best course is to listen to the insects and that their whole approach to the situation is far more sensible than the human approach; while the insects' instincts and approach are geared toward survival, both theirs' and man's, the human approach will lead toward destruction, not only of the insects but also of themselves. The second level of conflict, which provides the specific focus of much of the action and discussion in the novel, might be viewed as a political conflict that has several facets. One of these facets is the implicit conflict between those countries who have accepted the aims of the IEO and those countries which have rejected them; this conflict also includes the memory of past political conflicts, focused in the Chinese reaction to the years of exploitation by white imperialists. This is closely related to another facet, the manipulation of other countries through ideology and through the export of a set of techniques; this conflict is not particularly obvious, but it underlies many of the activities undertaken by Chen-Lhu. This, in turn, is also closely related to a third facet of the political conflict, the conflict between Chen-Lhu and Johnny Martinho, with Rhin Kelly in the center. In a sense, this facet is a personalization of the political relationship between China and Brazil; just as his government would use Brazil to further its aims and to lessen the impact of its failure in the realignment of insects, so too would Chen-Lhu use Johnny to further his own goals and to provide a scapegoat for the failure that is seen to be more and more inevitable as the novel progresses. Of course, these two levels of conflict are inseparable, for the primary political goals focused on in the novel are ecological ones, with all the manipulations focused on the way that the realignment process is going.

These conflicts begin working themselves out when insects linked into human form and function come to take Johnny and his father, an important political figure, to the brain, so that it might have direct contact, data, and a chance to convince them to try to change the course of events. His father has a heart attack, and Johnny is ordered by the insect-men to follow their directions. He panics when he sees the insects swarming over his father and he tries to get away, though they are deep in the jungle and in a place where the insects are strong. The only thing that saves him is the fact that they have ended up near the camp of Chen-Lhu, Rhin Kelly, and Johnny's group of bandeirantes; they use a protective foam to enable him to reach them. After a period of illness, which had struck the others earlier, Johnny, Chen-Lhu, and Rhin Kelly (she had been brought in by the IEO to seduce Johnny and set him up as the scapegoat) are chosen to take the pod, a self-enclosed, self-powered part of the bandeirante truck, down the river to find help. Just before they leave the camp, Chen-Lhu makes a remarkably candid (for him) statement of his purpose in the entire affair; in large measure, the journey which the three take down the river is a "fencing match" between the three that results from this confession. After they have left, the insects swarm over the camp, and orders have been given to keep watch over the three, to prevent others from finding them, and if at all possible to capture them alive. In the end, the insects do halt their progress, but before anything else can happen, Rhin kills Chen-Lhu, and, at her request, Johnny kills her and then himself rather than face the insects. However, the techniques which the insects have used to imitate, in a sense to become, humans can also be applied to specific parts of the body; just as his father's heart had been replaced by a symbiotic pump, so too are the damaged parts of Johnny and Rhin replaced. Although his father is extremely pleased by what the insects have done for him, and has been completely brought over to their cause, Johnny has severe doubts; he feels that he is no longer completely human and he feels that the course of action proposed will leave man the slave of the insects. The brain, however, ends the novel by suggesting that Johnny consider whether or not the sun is the slave of man — or of insect — simply because it supplies a life-necessity.

Thematically, then, the major thrust of the novel is pointing out the foolishness of ecological blindness. While it is true, for example, that many insects do eat food that humans might otherwise eat and do make things sometimes uncomfortable for humans, it is also true that without insects the land will become barren, unable to support any life at all. This point is made through Chen-Lhu's confession of what happened in China and through his suggestion that the same thing is happening in Brazil; it is explained in a brief lecture by the brain on the variety of functions served by insects, near the end of the novel. The novel also suggests that some kind of accommodation must be reached and that cooperation between insects and man is the only possible course, especially for human survival. Also included in these arguments is a persistent questioning of human motivations and assumptions; for the insects, survival is paramount, almost the only goal, while humans concern themselves with many other things, some of which, such as the realignment of insects and the power struggle between nations, tend very definitely in the direction of non-survival. Although in human affairs, ecological considerations must work through political institutions, the novel warns against letting the political aspects become overriding, become more important than survival. Thus, human survival is the central concern of *The Green Brain;* one aspect of man's current activities in relation to the world around him is projected, examined, and found wanting.

88

THE SANTAROGA BARRIER
1968

The Santaroga Barrier has a great deal in common with *Under Pressure,* although on the surface they would seem to be radically different. In both novels a psychologist, in the course of trying to solve a problem set for him by others, comes to a greater understanding of himself, of the society-in-miniature which he is studying, and of the larger society outside; in both novels, a psychologist is the central character and the course of his development is the primary focus of the novel, even though other elements are also explored. Finally, the basic structure of both novels is similar to a detective novel, with the hero undertaking the step-by-step discovery of the clues that will solve the mystery; although both novels share this structure, it is, however, much clearer and more central in *The Santaroga Barrier.*

The novel opens with Gilbert Dasein, a psychologist from the University of California at Berkeley, looking out over the Santaroga Valley. His purpose is to conduct a "market survey" of an unusual sort: a large chain store built a store in Santaroga which the natives of the valley refused to patronize, and the investment corporation behind the chain stores wants to know why; the whole problem is complicated by the fact that they admit that two earlier investigators had met accidental deaths in the valley (later, Dasein is informed that this figure was actually eight or nine). Furthermore, they have found that this "Santaroga Barrier" extends to nearly all relations between the Santarogans and those from the "outside": outsiders cannot find places to live in the valley, Santarogans report no juvenile delinquency or mental illness, all Santarogans who go outside the valley for the service or to college always return, and all outside investment is flatly rejected, and so on. Dasein must attempt to break through this barrier to find out what sets these people apart and how to get through to them. He is a good choice, since he had been very much involved with Jenny Sorgo, a Santarogan who had gone to Berkeley; the wonder of it is, as one of the natives points out, is that the investment corporation took so long to find him to do their job. He is, incidentally, sufficiently aware of his motivations to realize that the chance of seeing Jenny again is a major factor in his accepting the job.

He first feels the hostility of the natives when he comes into town, but the moment he indicates that he is acquainted with someone in the valley, he is quickly identified as Jenny's friend and the attitude changes rapidly. It does not take long for him to discover — to be told — that the Santarogans are willing and eager to recruit him, to bring him into the valley and make him one of them; in fact, there is evidence that Jenny may have been trying to do this while she was in college. Nevertheless, the first of a series of accidents befalls him the first night he spends in town, as he is nearly gassed in his room. This sets a pattern that follows throughout the novel; although the people seem to be very friendly and very cooperative (they know what he is after), nevertheless Gilbert undergoes a series of things that seem to be accidents but which also seem to defy the probabilities of that many accidents happening to one man, even to the most accident prone. These "accidents" provide him with another problem to solve: are they indeed accidents and, if they are not, what is causing them? Throughout the remainder of the novel, he gathers the clues that will answer these questions, as well as those he has been sent to find the answers to. The clues that he finds fall roughly into two categories, the biochemical and the sociological-psychological, while the answers also fall into the same categories, though with a heavier emphasis on the sociological-psychological.

The nature of Jaspers — a mysterious addictive substance — is the basis for the search along biochemical lines. That it is something other than simply the name of the locally made cheese is brought to Dasein's attention during his first meal in Santaroga; first, he tastes a distinct tang to his food, and then later the waiter, Winston Burdeaux, complains that the bartender won't allow Dasein to have more Jaspers beer. However, when he attempts to find out more about it from Burdeaux, he is put off and left without any information. Nevertheless, he gains some solid information about Jaspers, although he does not seem to find out exactly what it is or where it comes from; it might be noted that he insists on carrying out his investigation of this, as well as of everything else, the hard way, for he is suspicious of the Santarogans and unwilling to believe they will give him the full and truthful answer to his questions, although they say they will. One of the first things that he discovers is that Jaspers is "something" from the Co-op and that it is in nearly all the food and drink served in the valley to natives (they do, however, seem also to serve it to those they would like to recruit, a fact which the reader sees but Dasein does not). He finds out that somehow when food with Jaspers in it is taken out of the valley, the Jaspers disappears, and much later, near the end of the novel, he finds that light that is not in the red range affects it so that it disappears. Through a furtive excursion into the storage areas of the Co-op, he learns that people have lockers in which they expose various kinds of food to Jaspers; it might be noted that within a short time of the start of this excursion, many Santarogans know what he is doing and, rather than try to capture him, they are interested simply in knowing where he is. During the course of this excursion, Dasein, too, is exposed to Jaspers, to too much of it for someone who is not used to it; when he is told this, he also learns that he has been breathing it and that it has been entering his body through the pores. One of the results of this is the discovery that Jaspers seems to be addictive in a way; there is a craving reaction, and, when Santarogans leave the valley, they become much more sensitive to allergenic reactions. Another result is that Dasein begins to think in terms of drugs that heighten awareness; near the end of the novel, Dr. Piaget explains that, among other things, it speeds up the chemical action in the nervous system, breaks down blockage systems, and expands the mind's ability to formulate, all of which we see confirmed in Dasein's thoughts and actions. Shortly after he begins this thought process, he also makes the connection between what he calls zombie-like workers in the Co-op and an inability to accept and assimilate the changes produced by Jaspers. Another bit of information is added, when, on a picnic, he falls into the lake and nearly drowns; he finds that he has a heightened awareness of the processes of his body and that the Santa-rogans share an awareness of one another, a knowledge of the mood and attitude of those around them. Herbert is very careful at this point to note firmly that this awareness has nothing to do with telepathy. The final pieces of evidence are brought in while Dasein is in an isolation ward recovering from burns suffered in yet another accident. First, he finds that the effect of the Jaspers does fade and that the body recognizes this and acts to correct it. Second, Dr. Piaget explains about the speed-up of chemical reactions in the body. Third, he confirms the fact that the Jaspers is a kind of fungus growth with a thread-like spiral structure, and from Dr. Piaget he learns that the essence of Jaspers produces something yeastlike that is rich in amino acids and that the cells have no nucleus. Finally, he learns that Jaspers changes the body chemistry, making it more open to allergenic reactions when Jaspers are removed, but also improving hormone balance and speeding healing time so that it is five to ten times as fast as it would be without Jaspers.

These, then, are the facts about Jaspers; they do not add up to a particularly clear picture of the substance nor is there any clear discussion of how Jaspers produces its effects. Although this state of affairs bothers some readers of science fiction, it is probably best, for two reasons, that Herbert did not attempt a definitive description: 1.) to have done so would have invited full-scale comparison with current knowledge, which would indicate that we now have very little knowledge of what a substance with these properties would be like; and 2.) the major focus of *The Santaroga Barrier* is on the effects of this substance, on the social and psychological consequences of a change in conditions, so that a full-scale probing of the nature of Jaspers would be a misplaced emphasis and would get in the way of the central concerns of the novel. It might be noted at this point that in *Dune* the spice melange seems to have many of the same kinds of effects as Jaspers, indicating a continuing interest on the part of Herbert in altered states of consciousness. It might also be noted that there is very little explanation of melange provided in *Dune,* a fact which does not raise much comment; the feeling seems to be that by giving Jaspers as much attention as he did,

Herbert led the reader to expect something more along those lines than he delivered, whereas by taking melange more or less for granted as part of the general situation, he raised no such expectations. Whatever the case may be, however, all this information about the Jaspers provides the agent of change which alters human reactions to the world as we know it.

In a way similar to his gathering of information about Jaspers, Dasein also gathers information about the social structure of the valley and about the way they think about things. In this area, however, he comes to a larger conclusion and generalization about their way of life compared to life outside the valley, with the help of Dr. Piaget. Because there are so many details that go into this generalization and because they work smoothly toward his conclusion, it may be more helpful to begin with that generalization and work backward toward the particular details that are involved. Most important in this is his realization that the Santarogans are conservatives in the best sense of the word; they accept change when something genuinely better comes along, but they do not change simply for the sake of change and they preserve what is good and valuable from the past. Thus, they maintain language usages that are no longer used outside, they care for and improve upon older machinery, their social customs retain a flavor of an earlier era, their form of government is a basic democracy, many of their values seem not to have changed much over the years, and their buildings are old but sound and well kept, and so on. Another aspect of this conservativism is their concern for individuals as individuals; in the original sense of the word, a conservative was a person who stood for the rights of the individual as opposed to the rights of the state or federal governments, for the right of the individual to be his own man with minimal interference from others.

This respect for the individual also applies to Gilbert Dasein, although what we learn about the nature of his accidents and their probable causes would seem to negate this. Two factors seem to be most involved in these accidents. The first of these is the bond which the Santarogans share, the awareness of the emotions and attitudes of each individual in the valley, as well as the emotional ties with one another which this produces. The other is the fact that they unconsciously see all outsiders, but especially Dasein, as a threat to their survival; this becomes all the more important when it is recognized that a man who does not control his unconscious will use any means whatever to remove a threat to survival and that, while the Santarogans do deal with this in their training of the children, the training consists, apparently at least, of a form of repression of the unconscious urges rather than an integration of conscious and unconscious minds. Thus, repressed urges have a way of breaking out and manifesting themselves in subtle ways, in this case in creating situations which would lead to accidents for those who threaten the community's survival; this is accentuated by the shared bond, which would both intensify the threat through reinforcement of many minds and which would notify the group where Dasein is (they seem to be aware of him long before he is aware of them). It must be stressed that this "conspiracy" against Dasein is entirely unconscious and that they have *no* notion on the conscious level of what is happening. It is, for example, a great struggle for Dr. Piaget to even accept this as a possibility, and only Jenny seems to have had any glimpses of it; in fact, there seems to be a struggle involved even to remain aware of this. For example, by the end of the novel, Gilbert seems to have convinced himself that he had nothing to do with Selador's fall; this is a real disappointment and a flaw in the novel, since the reader had been led to believe that Dasein would be able to work with this problem. Nevertheless, on many levels, the Santoragans do seem to be genuinely committed to letting Gilbert do the job he was sent to do. They know what he is about, but there are no overt attempts to hinder his movements or his investigation; for example, although they know he is heading for the Jaspers storage areas, they make no attempt to stop him, though they do want to prevent overexposure. When he asks questions of Dr. Piaget, he is answered as truthfully as the doctor is able; a number of things that Piaget says are confirmed in other ways. In short, the Santarogans are as helpful as Dasein will allow them to be; in this, whatever they may do without conscious awareness, they are allowing Dasein the freedom to do what he must do as an individual.

All this is not to say, however, that there is not an area of conscious hostility to the world outside the valley, for there is. The Santarogans think of themselves as at war with the outside, more or less under siege from all directions (this, too, would reinforce their unconscious creation of accident situations). They feel that the outside world is dying, that outside a power struggle to control consciousness is taking place, that outsiders are destroying the environment, that outsiders accept all this passively, as spectators rather than as participants. This view is, in large part, responsible for their refusal to deal with the outside world in any way except those required for survival. Another part of the responsibility for this lies in the fact that they can sense the dichotomy between words and emotions and can see through the blandishments of advertising because of their Jaspers-heightened awareness. The reader gradually comes to accept the Santarogans' indictment of the outside world—our world—because Gilbert Dasein does; the reluctance and agony with which he accepts Santaroga as preferable to our world acts as a surrogate for the reader's reluctance to accept such an indictment. Once it is seen as an indictment, however, the ways in which life in the Santaroga Valley show up our own are many: they range from the shoddy way we build cars and care for them, to our passive addiction to television, to our treatment of the environment, to our power struggles, to our misleading advertising, and to our inter-personal relationships, as well as many other areas.

Although we may come to accept this indictment of our way of life, as Dasein does, and to believe that Santaroga offers a better alternative, our acceptance of the Santaroga society can never really be final, for it, too, is flawed. It, too, is either unwilling or unable to examine some of its assumptions and hidden motivations. As long as Dasein seems to be exploring and integrating the facets of his personality and to be aware of the source of the "accidents," the reader can feel that an adjustment can be made and the society become healthier; but when, at the inquest, he seems to absolve himself of responsibility for an accident, then the reader can no longer wholeheartedly accept the Santarogan way of life. Thus, although the novel and the society are flawed, *The Santaroga Barrier* nevertheless accomplishes what seems to be its main goal, forcing the reader to re-examine the way we live and the society we live in.

WHIPPING STAR
1970

Whipping Star seems to be the only Herbert novel which is related to a definitely separate short story; that is, while parts of other of his novels have first appeared as short stories before being incorporated into the novel, *Whipping Star* and "The Tactful Saboteur" bear no such relation. The short story is set some seventeen years before the action of *Whipping Star* and it introduces the characters of Napolean Bildoon and Jorj X. McKie, as well as detailing the history, purposes, and nature of the Bureau of Sabotage. Although Herbert also works this basic material into the novel in many and various ways, it will not be discussed here because of prior availability. As in "The Tactful Saboteur," the major focus in *Whipping Star* is on the attempt to establish real communication between two sentient species who perceive things in extremely different ways. Urgency is given to this attempt by the fact that most sentient life known to man may die unless such communication is established. All of these things combine to create an interesting story which is also one of the better science-fiction explorations of the problems of establishing real, mutually meaningful, communication between sentient forms of life.

The intelligent life form that is the focus of all this activity is a Caleban. At the beginning of the novel, very little is known about them, other than the facts that they "live" in hard spherical objects that they prefer to anchor in water, that no one has ever really seen one or established meaningful contact, and that they offered all beings the use of the S'eye Effect. The S'eye Effect, in practice, is a means of instantaneously moving from one place to another, no matter what the distance; it is obvious that a far-flung confederacy, such as that portrayed in this novel, would have great use for such a "device" but would fall apart if it were suddenly removed. Though it is extremely useful, no one in ConSent (the Confederacy of Sentients) understands what it is and how it works.

Another facet of the problem is that the Calebans have been disappearing without warning, somehow leaving a wake of insanity and death because they have left. Naturally, the government wants to know why and gives the problem to BuSab, which gives it on Jorj X. McKie. There is some feeling that this disappearance may be due to the fact that Mliss Abnethe has hired a Caleban so that she can indulge her sadistic urges and still avoid the laws of ConSent. Since BuSab is interested in this in its own right, it gives them a second reason to try to contact a Caleban.

Mliss Abnethe is an interesting case, as well as a thorn in the side of BuSab and Jorj X. McKie. She is an overwhelmingly rich woman who uses her money to get her own way in everthing. For example, when BuSab begins investigating, its agents find that her influence extends into many, many parts of the government, and to all levels. She can buy the best of legal, medical, and beauty care to maintain her and to prevent signs of aging, as well as protection against interference with her designs; in this last area, though, McKie proves to be slipperier than either her lawyers or her bodyguards. However, the aspect of Mliss Abnethe that is most important for this novel is her sado-masochism. That is, she has a long history of delight in inflicting pain on others. Although she has been treated for this condition, it only made her unable to bear the thought of pain in other sentients without removing the causes of her behavior; consequently, she is driven by contrary states of mind, accepting mental anguish in exchange for fulfillment of her need to inflict punishment. Thus, for her purposes, the Caleban is perfect, for it would be difficult to prove in a court of law that the Caleban suffers pain or that its idea of discontinuity equals death, and there *seems* to be no evidence that the contract between Abnethe and the Caleban is either involuntary or causing a public disturbance.

However, very early in his conversation with the Caleban, who gives herself the name Fanny Mae, she tells McKie that her home (the Beachball) contains the Master S'eye and that all sentients who have become entangled with her will share her fate if discontinuity overtakes her; then she explains that anyone who has used the S'eye "jumpdoors" has become entangled with her. Furthermore, Fanny Mae tells McKie that the floggings will cause her ultimate discontinuity after an indefinite number, but approximately ten, of further whippings. With this information, McKie and BuSab feel a sense of great urgency, and they might be able to move against Mliss Abnethe except for two problems: they need to establish more definitely that their interpretation of what the Caleban communicates is

accurate, and they need to find out just where Mliss is if they are to confront her in court.

These two problems, finding the location of Mliss Abnethe's hideway
and establishing accuracy of understanding between human and Caleban,
occupy McKie and other BuSab agents throughout the novel as they attempt to prevent the destruction of nearly all sentients, with gains in communication furthering their search for Mliss. The term which seems to
represent the difficulties of understanding is "connectives"; behind this
term, however, lie great differences in the ways Calebans and humans (and
other members of ConSent) perceive things. Eventually it becomes clear
that humans see things only on a single plane and in a strictly linear order,
whereas the Caleban seems to have all time and space laid out before it,
with intersections and nodes indicating points of contact between things,
beings, and events; the refined differences between these are the connectives. Once McKie begins to grasp this difference in perception and hence
the meaning of the term "connectives," he can go on to consider *what* a
Caleban is and how discontinuity might be prevented. It is, however, only
very near the end of the novel that McKie puts together several of the things
that Fanny Mae has said to realize that the Calebans manifest themselves
in this plane of existence as stars. Once he makes this connection, he then
also connects this with the idea that the Calebans seek energy here and that
this is somehow related to what is happening with the whippings. This is
verified electronically, and Fanny Mae is identified as the star known as
Thyone, in the Pleides, to humans. Then, McKie proceeds to the idea of
opening an immense "jumpdoor" into space so that Fanny Mae can ingest
great amounts of free hydrogen and thus replenish her substance. It also
leads to the realization that a Caleban manufactures emotion with its energy,
that they are nearly pure emotion and pure creativity, and that the whip
focused the emotion of hate behind it. With these realizations and the actions they bring about, the safety of great numbers of sentients is ensured,
as is the continuity of Thyone/Fanny Mae.

Although the evidence begins to pile up that Mliss Abnethe and her
followers are not to be found within the basic time-frame of the society, it is
only after McKie begins to understand the meanings of connectives that he,
first, and then others at BuSab, can begin to consider this as a serious
possibility. This evidence includes such things as McKie's journey to that
hideaway, where he sees Boers and blacks in a situation reminiscent of
late nineteenth and early twentieth century Africa. The analysis of the bull-
whip, the rope, and the sword they have gained also lead in this direction.
Nevertheless, the idea that the Caleban can see through space *and* time,
and thus can act in those "dimensions," is necessary before BuSab can begin to believe the possibility. However, further realizations—the fact that
the Calebans can perceive the psyche of other sentients, the fact that the

96

Calebans can "see" individuals to their real homes or to places they visualize, the fact that they are creative, and so on—refine this possibility. That is, the place where Mliss Abnethe *is* is the creation of her mind, her visualization of the Earth of the past, rather than actually existing in the past. It is the failure to realize *all* the implications of this, though he realizes some of them, that brings about the downfall of Abnethe's principle associate, Cheo, the ego-frozen Pan Spechi. Thus, he realizes that they do not exist in the real past but in a figment of Abnethe's imagination made real through the power of the Calebans; he does not, however, realize that Mliss is necessary to the contract with the Calebans and that her death will "discontinue" their existence. Or rather, he only begins to realize this when, on her death at his orders, the world begins to fade around him.

Although the search for Mliss Abnethe's hiding place provides nearly all of the action in the novel, it is the exploration of the difficulties of communication between species that defines the solution to the problems and that is the real focus of interest in the novel. It should be noted that this process of establishing mutual understanding is much more difficult than this discussion could possibly indicate, involving a great many attempts, a great many frustrations, and a great deal of intuition and good will; it is, after all, a process that takes the entire novel and results in broad understandings but very little detail. It might also be noted that, although we have no Calebans and no other sentient species to try to communicate with, this problem is a current problem, for it is quite firmly established that different languages (for example, English and Chinese or Russian) also imply different ways of viewing things; therefore, we, as Jorj X. McKie did, must learn not only the words of another language but also the perceptual system behind them if we are to achieve real communications with other human beings. Just as McKie's world's survival depended on his achieving such communication, so also does our world's survival depend on achieving real communication.

HELLSTROM'S HIVE
1973

One aspect of *Hellstrom's Hive* takes its inspiration from the film *The Hellstrom Chronicle*. The major focus of this aspect is the character of the narrator of that film, Nils Hellstrom, who not only is an expert on insects but is also very much impressed by their ability to survive—no matter what man or nature confronts them with. Whereas a novel such as *The Green Brain* points toward some kind of cooperation between man and insect, *Hellstrom's Hive* explores the possibilities of a human society imitating insect society, including genetic differentiation for the various roles and also including modifications that keeps it a human society. It is precisely because Nils Hellstrom is a product of just such an experimental society that he knows insects and admires them. The other major aspect of this novel is the attempted intrusion of powerful outside interests into the unique sub-society that has remained to itself for the most part; in this, *Hellstrom's Hive* has a great deal in common with *The Santaroga Barrier*. In both cases, for example, the intrusion is at the instigation of Big Business, although in *Hellstrom's Hive* this is somewhat masked by the fact that a government agency is the front for this activity, with the mention of the profit motive alone allowing penetration of this mask. Furthermore, both novels treat these sub-societies as ecological systems, with interactions on many levels between the members, including communication that approaches telepathy but is not—and what might be called the survival instinct. Although both societies have rejected the values, goals, and lifestyles of the larger society, both also have extensive contacts with the Outside and both recruit new members and new genetic patterns whenever possible. To a large extent, the main differences between these two sub-societies are the result of the differences in their sources of inspiration and uniqueness: where the hive society of *Hellstrom's Hive* is the result of deliberate choice and deliberate breeding, the conservative society of *The Santaroga Barrier* is the result of the consumption of a local fungus which has mind-expanding properties, apparently accidentally in the beginning, but deliberately once the cause and many of the effects are known.

Because both novels focus on Outsiders trying to find out more about the sub-society, they also share a similar structure built around those attempts; not only does this provide action-sequences for the novels but also it provides a gradual means for providing information about those societies. However, the fact that Herbert used a single psychologist-detective in *The Santaroga Barrier* allowed a greater emphasis on that individual and on his findings as he explored the lives of the people in the Santaroga Valley; the fact that he could gain access because of his relationship with one of the natives also helped focus on the society itself. In *Hellstrom's Hive,* on the other hand, it is a government agency with *teams* of men who are trying to gain access, which they cannot do easily. As a result, there is a dual focus in this novel, one on the machinations of the government agency as it tries to find out what is going on at the Hellstrom farm, the other on the hive society as it gears up to meet this potential threat to its survival. It is, of course, this dual focus and the conflict, both spoken and unspoken, between the two groups that provides the dramatic tension of the novel.

The Agency—the only name given it in the novel—becomes interested in Nils Hellstrom and his various activities when they discover a file folder with partial information on something labelled Project-40 on a library table at MIT, carelessly left there for a short time by one of the members of his filming crew. They check this information out and find that it is, from what can be seen from incomplete data, both something new and a valid direction of research; although there are indications that this is a weapon, they dismiss this and concentrate on its potentials for revolutionizing metallurgy. At the same time that they send this information to experts to decipher and pursue, they also begin to try find out more about Hellstrom and about the farm which is the center of his movie-making operations. When their first operative, Porter, does not return after making several reports that indicate something odd about the farm, they send out the team of Carlos Depeaux and Tymiena Grinelli. When they, too, fail to return, several things happen at the Agency. First, Dzule Peruge, the second man in the hierarchy, with the consent of the Chief (later identified as Altman when he commits suicide), begins to set Joseph Merrivale, the director of operations, up as a scapegoat in case anything should go wrong. Second, Peruge sets up operations so that he will lead a more substantial force in the field; Merrivale, of course, begins to cover himself by assigning Shorty Janvert to be second in command. In addition, the board of control (whose members are never identified either by name or by position) exhibits some impatience at the lack of information that has been developed concerning Hellstrom, which provides an added goad to Peruge. At about this point in the novel, Herbert takes some time to characterize Peruge as a man who has gravitated to the Agency because he is a romantic adventurer and who hopes to become rich from what he uncovers on this mission. However, Peruge meets a blank wall when he approaches Hellstrom, partly because Hellstrom has had some time to prepare, but more because Hellstrom had not realized the metallurgical possibilities of Project 40. Before this can be carried much further, Fancy, one of the hive's top line of females, seduces Peruge; as a result, he dies of a heart attack, caused by too much sexual activity. This in turn brings Shorty Janvert to the farm, who takes a hard line about reinforcements coming in. Especially when he does not return, Clovis Carr and other members of the team come in shooting; all are either killed or captured. About this time, the Chief commits suicide and Merrivale arrives on the scene, apparently committed to escalating the attack. However, he must now depend on the support of other agencies, most notably the FBI; they are willing to help only as long as the Agency's assessment of the situation can be accepted as correct. By the time all of this has transpired, work on Project 40 has been completed, and the hive has the means to hold off further threats, at least for the time being. Even though a certain weapon could destroy the entire world, or any selected part of it. Merrivale is ready to send in bombs; fortunately, cooler heads finally overrule him and suggest open bargaining with Hellstrom.

Even though Merrivale's actions at the end are overdone and rather melodramatic, this portrait of the government is not a pretty one, with power misused in a number of ways. Although the nature of the Agency is never clearly specified, three things about it seem to stand out: it is a secret agency of the government, it has a direct line to the President, and it is controlled by a group of people interested in information and profit. Its methods are, of course, covert; they seem to feel that it is their right to get any information they want and to feel angry when obstacles are put in their path, and they are willing to use any means necessary to get what they are after. Nevertheless, it does not seem accurate to call the larger society in this novel a police state. For one thing, the Agency has limits on what it can do and is not all-powerful. In addition, although the Agency does not have set rules to follow, such agencies as the FBI do; these other agencies will support the Agency to a certain point and then only as long as the Agency's assessment of a situation can be defended. Finally, the ending of the novel makes it quite clear that, at least in the Hellstrom case, further action by the Agency, or at its request, has been halted. Nevertheless, even though this society may not be a police state, it is well on the way toward becoming one. Recent revelations of the uses, and attempted uses, of government agencies for purposes other than their functions suggest that we are not far from the society Herbert describes in this novel.

Because the major emphasis of *Hellstrom's Hive* is this threat from the government and the ways in which the hive moves to meet the threat, much of what the reader learns of this hive society is rather indirect. The roots of the hive go back several centuries to Europe, with several references to beginnings three hundred years earlier (the time of the novel is late twentieth century, probably the 1970s); specific impetus was apparently given by the work of Gregor Mendel and by a move from Europe to America in the late nineteenth century. This move brought the group to Guarded Valley in southeastern Oregon. There, using a natural cavern as a beginning point, they began expanding their colony downward, until the colony extends over a mile downward and outward in a circle two miles in diameter. In this area, there are approximately 50,000 human beings and many of the supporting elements for life—hydroponic gardens, power generators, laboratories, living quarters, medical facilities, factories, and so on. However, not all the things needed for life and expansion are possible in the hive; this is one reason that Hellstrom operates the film company, to gain the money necessary for those things which they cannot yet produce themselves. The other primary reason is the desire to prepare the groundwork for eventual expansion of the hive concept throughout the world, to begin people thinking along those lines.

Within the hive, everything is functional. Perhaps the thing which shocks most people about this concept of society is the functionalization of humans. The largest segment of the population in this society are the workers, the people who do all the required labor, maintenance, and other such tasks; these workers are not only specifically bred and trained for the jobs they are to do, but they are also fed a specific diet designed to help them function well. Beyond these workers are a number of specialists, also bred, trained, and fed according to the types of work they must do. For example, there are the researchers, bred for intellect and delicate manipulation. There are security specialists, bred for intelligence, caution, and imagination, and trained to protect the hive in a variety of ways. There are also leaders, such as Hellstrom, as well as many others filling necessary functions throughout the operation of the hive. It might be noted that there is rarely any confusion in the activities of the hive, for each person has a precise place and a precise function to fill, and each has been trained to fill it well. In addition, in keeping with the constant alertness of the hive to avoid becoming too thoroughly like the insects they emulate, there is a much greater range of specialists than there would be in an insect hive. In this sense, there is not a great deal of difference between the hive and the world outside; in the outside world, there are also the workers and the specialists, but they find such roles in a helter-skelter fashion that is often wasteful and non-productive. Another facet of this society, which is also a product of breeding, training, and feeding, is its great solidarity, particularly in defense of the hive; there is a recognition of everyone belonging to the hive because of body chemistry and there is a tremendous drive to keep the hive safe from intruders and from any danger. There are also dangers in this, for this drive to defend is difficult to control and any excitement in any part of the hive quickly spreads to the rest of the hive, thus creating two problems instead of one. Nevertheless, in spite of the momentary confusion at the height of the attack, the hive functions smoothly in all situations, aiming always at the advancement and survival of the hive.

On the whole, the attitude of the novel toward the hive society is ambivalent. Obviously, Hellstrom and his associates are convinced that this is an alternative to current society that will ultimately overcome it; this is supported by many of the passages from diaries and so on. Just as obviously, Merrivale and many of his associates feel the hive to be an abomination to be utterly and totally destroyed in any way possible. There is very little middle ground; only Clovis Carr and Shorty Janvert seem to make the movement from one side of the conflict to the other, but any commitment they make is not clearly indicated in the novel itself. In addition, there is the question of whether their choice is made because they have become convinced that hive life is better or simply because it will allow them to do things they couldn't do outside. Finally, although it is easy to admit that the larger society is not at all desirable, there is really very little effort made to make the hive society particularly attractive as an alternative; in fact, many of the aspects of the hive will seem repulsive to many readers. In the last analysis, the main purpose of the novel seems to be simply to hold this alternative up for the reader's contemplation, with little urging either toward acceptance or rejection; any choice is strictly the reader's own.

Hellstrom's Hive, then, deals with three themes that recur throughout Herbert's works: 1) the misuse of governmental powers; 2) the exploration of a society that is alternative to our own; and 3) a look at ecology, with special attention to the place of human beings within the ecology and to an ecology of human beings. Because a major focus is on the intrusions of the Agency, the novel reads rather like a spy-thriller; because the society proposed is unique and the spy-thriller aspect quite common, one might wish that the exploration of the society had been given more direct attention. Nevertheless, Herbert made a choice of approach. Within the limits of that choice, the reader does get a solid exploration of his main themes, making the novel both interesting and provocative.

NOTES

NOTES

NOTES